Sunday

after

Sunday

Sunday
after
Sunday

Preaching the Homily as Story

Robert P. Waznak, S.S.

Paulist Press *New York/Ramsey*

Library of Congress Catalog Card Number: 82-62922

ISBN: 0-8091-2540-4

Published by Paulist Press
545 Island Road, Ramsey, N.J. 07446

Printed and bound in the United States of America

Contents

for three friends who listened
Monday after Monday:
Melvin C. Blanchette, S.S.
David M. Carey
Edward J. Frazer, S.S.

Introduction

What does it mean to preach? An ancient metaphor provides a definition: "to wrestle with God's Word." The word "wrestle" is crucial. No authentic preacher thinks it is a breeze. St. Paul told the Corinthians that when he came to preach Jesus Christ to them, "it was in weakness and in fear, and with much trepidation" (1 Cor 2:3).

To preach once is not too difficult a contest. Most believers can preach an effective homily once in their lives. They can tell their own story of God that makes sense and gives hope to our own story. But the preacher is called to do this Sunday after Sunday. That is where the wrestling begins—the ongoing match with God's Word that demands work, humility, and creativity.

Sunday after Sunday preaching is demanding, especially in the post-Vatican II Church. Prior to the Council, Catholic tradition did not insist upon the centrality of preaching as the Reformed churches did. In catechism class we rattled off "the three most important parts of the Mass: Offertory, Consecration and Communion." To fulfill one's obligation for Mass, one had to be present from the time of the Offertory or, to be even more specific, from the moment the priest removed the veil from the chalice. Such thinking revealed our appreciation of the liturgy of the Word. It showed how far we had come from St. Augustine's reflection that "the Word of God is not less important than the Body of Christ." Just a few years before the Council, one Catholic author wrote:

> The sermon is accidental to the Mass, and although it is important, its omission does not affect the integrity of the great act of worship. . . . Consequently, if the priest feels, for one reason or another, that a choice must be made between Mass and the sermon, obviously there is no choice—the Mass takes precedence.[1]

Vatican II sought to change this manner of thinking and return to the ancient understanding of the homily as an integral link between the service of the Word and the Eucharist. This renewal is reflected in the *Constitution on the Sacred Liturgy* which insists on the "intimate connection between words and rites" and refers to the homily not as accidental but as "part of the liturgy itself" that is to be preached "with exactitude and fidelity" (Arts. 35, 52). The followup *Instruction* (1964) insists that "there shall be a homily on Sundays and feasts of precept in all Masses which are celebrated with the people present. No exception may be made for conventual, sung, or pontifical Masses" (Art. 53). In the past, exceptions had often been made to drop the homily from the Mass. As a boy I remember our pastor announcing on an early Sunday in June: "Next Sunday we will begin our summer schedule" which we all knew meant no sermon until after Labor Day.

Another note of the priority of preaching in the Council's documents is found in the *Decree on the Ministry and Life of Priests* which states: "Priests, as co-workers with their bishops, have as their primary duty the proclamation of the Gospel of God to all" (Art. 4).

Not only did Vatican II declare the centrality of preaching, but it called for a different style of preaching. There was to be a restoration of the liturgical homily of the early Church which proclaimed the fact that God has acted and continues to act in our lives. This proclamation was to arise from the scriptural texts in the liturgy of the day and was to be addressed to the particular needs of the congregation. The homily was not to be used primarily as a mode for instruction or moralizing but as a proclamation of the good news. The homily was not to be drawn from sermon plans that had no connection with the Scripture readings of the Mass. A new cycle of scriptural readings gave a new challenge to preach God's Word in a language that made sense to a new age. The *Decree on the Ministry and Life of Priests* states:

> If it is to influence the mind of the listener more fruitfully, such preaching must not present God's Word in a general and abstract fashion only, but it must apply the perennial truth of the Gospel to the concrete circumstances of life (Art. 4).

An example of how we have grown since the Council in our awareness of the centrality of a new kind of preaching is found in a letter of the Catholic bishop of Pittsburgh to his priests:

> Homily preparation is one of the main occupations of the priest. It should be considered an integral, necessary aspect of his spiritual life. . . . It demands time for actual composition and some consideration of the style of delivery. In short, the preparation of the Sunday homily holds a priority in his weekly schedule.[2]

There are hopeful signs that many preachers are taking their pulpit ministry seriously. Some are enrolled in preaching courses and workshops. Many prayerfully study and reflect on the Sunday readings with others and with the use of new homily aids.

Despite these efforts to continue the wrestling of God's Word, research shows that there is a growing dissatisfaction among the people with the quality of preaching. In his recent study of American Catholics, Andrew W. Greeley writes that only twenty-five percent of Catholics rate homilies "excellent" (twelve percent for those under thirty).[3] Greeley concludes: "The quality of sermons, in other words, must be considered an important correlate of Catholic religious involvement—more important than clericalism, feminism, racism, and in some respects even more important than sexual attitudes."[4]

Many preachers are beginning to realize that people are accustomed to new and creative styles of communication from our media-packed society and that their listeners are also wrestling with God's Word to discern how it might affect the practical events of their lives. Preachers sense that the contemporary search for self-fulfillment, the liberation of the human spirit, and the expectation of honesty from leaders are all pressing hard upon the Sunday homily. Many preachers suspect that their theological and biblical training has become inadequate in a post-Vatican II Church. That is why priests selecting topics from their diocesan institutes and workshops are choosing preaching as a top priority. That is why preachers are searching out homiletic services to help update their homilies. Many preachers are beginning to grasp that information about God is not enough, that an experience of God is what seems lacking.

How do we begin to put these concerns, criticisms, and needs in perspective? How do we continue to wrestle with God's Word in the modern arena?

To help answer these questions, a sobering sense of history is critical. To think that disfavor of preaching is a new wind swept into the open windows of a post-Vatican II Church simply is not true. Nowhere in the history of the Church did Christians shout with wide acclaim: "Preaching is great these days!" In fact, a solid case can be made for the opposite. Blunt criticisms can be found even in the early Church. St. Paul quotes one of his listeners in Corinth: "His letters, they say, are severe and forceful, but when he is here in person he is unimpressive and his word makes no great impact" (2 Cor 10:10). The Middle Ages witnessed a time of dull and shallow preaching which was frequently a repetition of earlier homilies. In one of the most popular services of the day, Johannes de Werden (1437) writes in the preface of his *Dormi Secure:* "Sleep soundly and don't worry about your sermon tomorrow; there are plenty to choose from in the book."[5] In the nineteenth century, which some have called the "golden age of preaching," N. M. Neal comments:

> . . . the same same Sunday always producing the same sermon. Whatever might be the circumstances of the hearers . . . the priest never able to appeal to local events, home occurrences, anything, in short, that could touch and interest the instructor: and the sermons so evolved as unintelligible as if they had been written in Latin.[6]

And if you think Protestants, who have proudly advocated the primacy of preaching, have been immune to criticism, just read Clyde E. Fant's list of twentieth century magazine articles on the pulpit, which includes such gloomy titles as "Why Sermons Make Us Go To Sleep" (1908), "Is Preaching Obsolete?" (1911), "The Futility of Sermons" (1925), and "A Halt to Preaching" (1936).[7]

In short, preaching has always been a sore spot in the Church. Preachers and people have often walked away from the pulpit with heavy hearts. And yet there is a sense in which each age in the Church can be called a golden age of preaching because some preachers have continued the wrestling, lifting hearts and minds with the good news in the midst of the bad. Listen to the story of Payne Best, a British secret service agent who described Dietrich Bonhoeffer's sermon on April 8, 1945, as a small group of prisoners in a Nazi cell begged Bonhoeffer to conduct a worship service since they feared the end was near:

> Pastor Bonhoeffer held a little service and spoke to us in a manner which reached the hearts of all, finding just the right words to express the spirit of our imprisonment and thoughts and resolutions which it has brought.[8]

While Bonhoeffer's last sermon was a unique and dramatic event, all of us who have wrestled with God's Word have known those times when the homily "reached the hearts of all, finding just the right words to express the spirit of our imprisonment and the thoughts and resolutions which it has brought." From majestic cathedrals to simple living room liturgies, the language of the Bible was somehow translated into the language of the people which made the listeners walk away with hope and the preachers with a conviction that the wrestling must continue.

What needs to be done is not to substitute the preacher with a slide show nor to write another article on the disenchantment of preaching nor to blindly walk backward to model some mythical golden age of preaching. We must continue the wrestling in our own time in a way that is both hopeful and honest. We should look to the current criticism of our homilies not as reasons for despair but as a rich source for improvement where we can respond humbly to the needs of God's people. As Pope Paul VI said in an address in September 1975:

> If the faith is failing to find hearers and believers, is this because it is taught and preached in an old, abstrusive way, cut off from life and contrary to the tendencies and tasks of today? Ought we not renew the kerygma—the announcement of the Christian message—if we want to find hearers and followers?[9]

One way I have chosen to continue the wrestling with God's Word is by offering these reflections on what it means to preach Sunday after Sunday in the post-Vatican II Church.

Since the Council, serious and creative steps have been taken in seminaries to upgrade homilectic courses. The use of video-tape equipment for feedback, the small group process where a student receives professional and peer criticism, the experience of preaching often in class and to "real" congregations, and the integration of preaching with Scripture and theology courses are all indications of the homiletic upgrading.

Yet, it seems that something still is lacking. It may help to explain what I mean by pointing to Benjamin S. Bloom's *Taxonomy of Education Objectives* that outlines three significant domains of education: the *cognitive* where information is received and exchanged, the *attitudinal* where attitudes are formed and exchanged, and the *performances* domain where a student acquires certain skills.[10] While it seems that we have made some strides in the performance domain of homiletic courses, the attitudinal and the cognitive domains often have been neglected. It is not enough to teach a student *how* to preach (performance); we must provide the creative educational experience of *why* (attitudinal) and *what* (cognitive) we preach so that the student can build upon these experiences over the years in ministry.

This book, therefore, is designed to help us to reflect on three main goals of preaching:

(1) *Cognitive,* to offer an interpretation of life based on the biblical view which calls for an awareness of who we are and who we are called to be. It is an interpretation that orders the events of our life with a vision, a way of "seeing in the dark."

(2) *Attitudinal,* to invite people to a change of heart, to confront the comfortable and comfort the afflicted. This conversion experience is ongoing and is found in our liturgical tradition of the homily envisioned by the renewal of Vatican II. The homily is a proclamation of the good news which invites people to thanksgiving and conversion not only at the Eucharistic table, but also in our personal and social choices of life.

(3) *Performance,* to offer people not just a skilled performance in the pulpit, but a caring ministry. Basic performance skills such as effective eye contact, appropriate body language, and voice projection and variation, vital to effective preaching, are not touched upon in this text. An attempt is made, however, to present a homily with a "planned spontaneity": a technique which emphasizes a storylike quality for preaching.

This book is designed to fill some gaps in contemporary Catholic homiletics by providing an overview of the renewal of preaching ushered in by Vatican II, plus some theoretical and practical observations on wrestling with God's Word, Sunday after Sunday in today's world.

I am grateful for the critical suggestions of my colleagues at the Washington Theological Union, especially Rick Duhn, and at St. Mary's Seminary in Baltimore, especially David

Murphy, Patricia Parachini, S.N.J.M., and Thomas Hurst, S.S. I am indebted to my friends in the pews who helped shape these reflections, especially the congregation at the old Basilica in Baltimore. Lastly, I thank Tim Pierce for his special help and David Bowlin who typed the manuscript.

RPW
Advent 1982

I

The Homily

For many Catholics, the *aggiornamento* of Vatican II came with the catastrophic suddenness of an avalanche. But just as an avalanche does not commence without a previous long, maturing thaw, the Council was really the culmination of a renewal that had been in preparation for decades.

Nowhere was this more true than in the worship of the Church. For many Catholics, such liturgical changes as priests facing the people as they celebrated the Eucharist, the Mass in the vernacular, and active participation by the congregation in the liturgy appeared new and strange. Yet, these innovations were the natural result of two scholarly endeavors that had been in progress for many years: the biblical and liturgical movements.

Biblical Movement

The scientific, critical study of the Bible that appeared in Catholic circles at the end of the nineteenth century received papal approbation in Pius XII's *Divino Afflante Spiritu* in 1943. The fruits of modern methods of interpretation of the Scriptures inaugurated by this encyclical are found throughout the sixteen documents of the Second Vatican Council. Oscar Cullmann remarks here that the "Catholic Church in Vatican II not only goes back behind the Counter-Reformation, but even behind the Middle Ages. It goes back to the Bible."[1]

Liturgical Movement

A vigorous and scholarly liturgical movement pioneered in the monasteries of such northern European countries as Holland, Belgium, France, and Germany at the beginning of this century was articulated in *Mediator Dei* by Pius XII (1947). This encyclical and the research of modern biblical criticism helped provide a liturgical and theological framework for Vatican II's document on the sacred liturgy.

As a measure of its significance in the life of the Church, the *Constituion on the Sacred Liturgy* (hereinafter referred to as *S.L.*) was the first constitution published by the Council (December 4, 1963). This doctrinal and disciplinary decree has been acclaimed "the most important document for the life of the Church since the sixteenth century."[2] Since preaching is intimately linked with the Church's worship, *S.L.* specifically presented a program of homiletic renewal.

Catholic Preaching Prior to Vatican II

While the Catholic Church did not discover preaching at the Second Vatican Council, it did insist on a new style of preaching.

Catholics had been accustomed to sermons that had little to do with the liturgical context in which they were preached. Frank B. Norris, describing Catholic preaching prior to Vatican II, writes:

> We've heard many "sermons on the Gospel," but at least frequently these have amounted to not much more than a retelling of the Gospel story with appropriate moral exhortations. We are also accustomed to topical sermons, the context of which would be largely dogmatic, moral, sociopolitical, or hagiographical, as the case may be. We may even have been officially instructed to preach sermons of a topical nature (according to a given outline) in series which would last for a year or even longer.[3]

There is a sense in which the sermon was regarded as an interruption of the Mass instead of an integral part of the worship. William O'Shea described the worship sermon before Vatican II:

> Cut off from the liturgical action which it once developed and explained, the sermon developed into an independent and autonomous activity having no relation to anything else, much less to worship. The very content of preaching changed. From a proclamation of the Word of God (as it was in apostolic and patristic times) it became—and largely has remained—a thinly-disguised classroom lecture. More often than not it has little of the doctrinal about it, and is confined mostly to moral exhortation.[4]

The Loss of the Homiletic Ideal of the Primitive Church

The homily, which in the early Church expounded the Scripture readings of the liturgy and encouraged participation in the Eucharist, gradually lost these liturgical functions in the Middle Ages. The homily became a speech independent of the liturgy. In fact, the monumental homilectic treatise *De Eruditione Praedicatorum* by Humbert of Romans (d. 1277) does not even mention the homily in the context of liturgical preaching. The medieval pulpit often became a platform for Scholastic speeches, denunciations of heresies and recitations of fantastic tales and fables. The independence of the homily from the actual celebration of the Mass is even reflected in the Church architecture of the time, where the pulpit came into prominence outside the area of the sanctuary.

The Counter-Reformation's renewal of preaching did not seek to restore the liturgical homily of the primitive Church, but adopted the sermon as an educational channel for the teachings of the Council of Trent. Moral and dogmatic sermons were presented in defense of the Catholic faith. A place was left in the liturgy for the sermon, but it was not always directly related to the Scripture readings of the Mass of the day. Prior to Vatican II, many dioceses provided homiletic syllabi containing various religious topics that were totally unrelated to the scriptural readings of the Mass. There were times when authors attempted to make some link between the topic and the Scripture readings, but most often this meant stretching the readings to fit a pre-conceived series of doctrinal topics.

The homiletic renewal of Vatican II clearly manifests a change from the traditional topical sermon to the ancient liturgical homily. The importance of this shift cannot be underestimated. In the primitive Church, in other words, preaching was a clear and definitive part of the total worship service. It was part of the liturgy itself, and drew its themes from the Mass itself. By the time of Humbert of Romans in the thirteenth century, however, this was not always true.

Vatican II represents a clearly definable point of change and a return to the spirit of the ancient liturgical homily. This shift is indeed identifiable and is reinforced by certain passages from *S.L.* and from other constitutions of Vatican II that deal specifically with a renewal of preaching. This documentation manifests the two dominant themes of scriptural and liturgical renewal, besides the other themes that are pertinent for a clear understanding of contemporary Catholic homiletics.

The Homiletic Teachings of Vatican II

Importance of Preaching

The Council sought to renew preaching by emphasizing its importance in the life of the Church. The *Dogmatic Constitution on the Church* (Art. 25) states:

Among the principal duties of bishops, the preaching of the Gospel occupies an eminent place. For bishops are preachers of the faith who lead new disciples to Christ. They are authentic teachers, that is, teachers endowed with the authority of Christ, who preach to the people committed to them the faith they must believe and put into practice.

The Council's *Decree on the Ministry and Life of Priests* (Art. 4) also stressed the significance of preaching in the ministry:

> The people of God finds its unity first of all through the Word of the living God, which is quite properly sought from the lips of priests. Since no one can be saved who has not first believed, priests, as co-workers with their bishops, have as their primary duty the proclamation of the Gospel of God to all. In this way they fulfill the Lord's command: "Go into the whole world and preach the Gospel to every creature" (Mk 16:15). Thus they establish and build up the people of God.

To implement the Council's homiletic task, the *Decree on Priestly Formation* (Art. 19) insists:

> That pastoral concern which should thoroughly penetrate the entire training of seminarians also requires that they be carefully instructed in those matters which have a special bearing on the sacred ministry, especially catechetics, preaching, liturgical worship, the conferral of the sacraments, works of charity, the duty of seeking out the straying sheep and unbelievers, and other pastoral obligations.

Finally, in the *Decree on the Missionary Activity of the Church* (Art. 6) the Council emphasized the importance of preaching in the ministry of evangelization:

> The chief means of this implantation is the preaching of the Gospel of Jesus Christ. The Lord sent forth his disciples into the whole world to preach this Gospel. Thus, reborn by the Word of God (cf. 1 Pet 1:23), men may through baptism be joined to that Christ which, as the body of the Word Incarnate, is nourished and lives by the Word of God and by the Eucharistic bread (cf. Acts 2:43).

Preaching and Scripture

The Council made it clear that Scripture should be a primary source for preaching. The *Dogmatic Constitution on Divine Revelation* (Art. 21) states:

> Therefore, like the Christian religion itself, all the preaching of the Church must be nourished and ruled by sacred Scripture. For in the sacred books, the Father who is in heaven meets His children with great love and speaks with them.

And in *S.L.* (Art. 24) we read:

> Sacred Scripture is of paramount importance in the celebration of the liturgy. For it is from Scripture that lessons are read and explained in the homily, and psalms are sung; the prayers, collects and liturgical songs are scriptural in their inspiration, and it is from Scripture that actions and signs derive their meaning.

Preaching and Religious Education

In the Council documents, preaching is seen as an indispensable channel for the instruction of Christian doctrine. Speaking of the teaching duty of bishops in the *Decree on the Bishops' Pastoral Office in the Church* (Art. 13), we read:

> They should also strive to use the various means at hand today for making Christian doctrine known: namely, first of all, preaching and catechetical instruction which always hold pride of place.

The same document (Art. 30) speaks of the duty of pastors:

> In the exercise of their teaching office, it is the duty of pastors to preach God's Word to all the Christian people so that, rooted in faith, hope and charity, they may grow in Christ and the Christian community may bear witness to that charity which the Lord commended.

Preaching and Relevance

The Council believed that effective preaching in today's world called for a practical homiletics that made the Gospel relevant to the needs and aspirations of contemporary men and women. In the *Decree on the Ministry and Life of Priests* (Art. 4), the following advice is given:

> No doubt, priestly preaching is often very difficult in the circumstances of the modern world. If it is to influence the mind of the listener more fruitfully, such preaching must not present God's Word in a general and abstract fashion only, but it must apply the perennial truth of the Gospel to the concrete circumstances of life.

Preaching and the Liturgy

While one can locate evidence of a renewal of preaching throughout the documents of the Second Vatican Council, the most specific program for homiletic renewal is found in *S.L.* It is here that the Council spells out the new kind of preaching that is expected of preachers—the liturgical homily:

> 35. That the intimate connection between words and rites may be apparent in the liturgy:
>
> (1) In sacred celebrations there is to be more reading from Holy Scripture, and it is to be more varied and suitable.
>
> (2) Since the sermon is part of the liturgical service, the preferred place for it is to be indicated even in the rubrics, as far as the nature of the rite will allow; and the ministry of preaching is to be fulfilled with exactitude and fidelity. The sermon, moreover, should draw its content mainly from scriptural and liturgical sources. Its character should be that of a proclamation of God's wonderful work in the history of salvation, that is, the mystery of Christ, which is ever made present and active within us, especially in the celebration of the liturgy.
>
> 52. By means of the homily the mysteries of the faith and the guiding principles of the Christian life are expound-

ed from the sacred text during the course of the liturgical year. The homily, therefore, is to be highly esteemed as part of the liturgy itself; in fact, at those Masses which are celebrated with the assistance of the people on Sundays and feasts of obligation, it should not be omitted except for a serious reason.

To implement the Council's *aggiornamento* of liturgy, an instruction was promulgated September 20, 1964. *The Sacred Congregation of Rites Instruction for the Proper Implementation of the Constitution on the Sacred Liturgy* (hereinafter referred to as the *Instruction*) sheds further light on the Council's concept of the liturgical homily:

> 53. There shall be a homily on Sundays and feast days of precept, in all Masses which are celebrated with the people present. No exception may be made for conventual, sung, or pontifical Masses. On other days, a homily is recommended, especially some of the weekdays of Advent and Lent, as well as in other circumstances when the people come to church in larger numbers.

> 54. By a homily from the sacred text is understood an explanation either of some aspect of the readings from Holy Scripture or of another text from the Ordinary or Proper of the Mass of the day, taking into account the mystery which is being celebrated and the particular needs of the hearers.

> 55. If plans of preaching within Mass are proposed for certain periods, the intimate connection with at least the principal seasons and feasts of the liturgical year (cf. Constitution, Arts. 102–104), that is, with the mystery of the Redemption, is to be harmoniously preserved: for the homily is part of the liturgy of the day.

The preceding documentation from Vatican II demonstrates the importance that was assigned to preaching, the educational benefits of preaching and the insistence upon a new kind of preaching that is kerygmatic, liturgical, scriptural, and relevant.

An Interpretation of the Homiletic Teachings of Vatican II

The Homily

The word "sermon" is used in Art. 35 of *S.L.* It is significant, however, to note that the word "homily" is more frequently employed in this document (Art. 52) and in the *Instruction* (Arts. 53, 54, 55).

In the *Dogmatic Constitution on Divine Revelation,* a homily is a specific type of preaching that is highly esteemed:

> This ministry includes pastoral preaching, catechetics, and all other Christian instruction, among which the liturgical homily should have an exceptional place (Art. 24).

The significance of the liturgical homily also is found in *S.L.* (Art. 52) and the *Instruction* (Art. 53) which insists on the obligation of preachers to deliver liturgical homilies.

The word "homily" itself suggests a new kind of preaching in the Catholic community. In Catholic parlance, the word "sermon" now connotes pre-Vatican II preaching, while the word "homily" suggests the new kind of preaching promoted by the Council. This connotation of homily seems peculiar to Catholics. Most Protestant authors refer to homily as a way in which a preacher "walks through" the biblical text verse by verse. Richard A. Jensen, for example, describes homily as a "step by step unfolding of the text."[5] When Catholic authors refer to homily, they are not suggesting a verse-by-verse explanation of the biblical text, but that form of biblical and liturgical preaching ushered in by the reforms of Vatican II.

The word "homily" is derived from the Greek *homileo* which denotes a familiar conversation. Although the word "homily" did not exist until the patristic period and, therefore, does not appear in the New Testament, the word *homileo* is frequently used to denote an informal kind of preaching (cf. Acts 20:26; 24:26; Lk 24:14; 1 Cor 14:33).

William O'Shea has pointed out that the word "homily"

cannot be understood by a mere examination of the etymology of the word. "It must be understood in the light of its use in patristic times, when the homily grew up and developed."[6] It was Origen who first used the word "homily" in Christian preaching as a commentary on some biblical passage. He distinguished this familiar type of preaching from *logos* which was a formal sermon with exordium, body, and conclusion. Such sermons would include conferences, controversies, panegyrics, and apologies.

Another distinction seems appropriate here. Charles H. Dodd in *The Apostolic Preaching and Its Developments*[7] spoke of three kinds of preaching in the Christian tradition: (1) *kerygma* which refers to evangelical or missionary preaching like that of St. Peter in Acts 10:42; (2) *paraclesis* which is a preaching that continues the conversion of those who have accepted the *kerygma;* the Epistle to the Hebrews is an example of *paraclesis;* (3) *didache* which is an explanation of the Christian doctrine; this kind of preaching is continued today in pre-Cana instructions, C.C.D. classes, parish discussion clubs, and Sunday schools. A liturgical homily would best fit Dodd's category of *paraclesis,* since it is a discourse delivered to those who have already committed themselves to the good news and come to be further nourished by the good news at the community's celebration of the Eucharist.

S.L. does not rule out what Dodd has called *kerygma* or *didache* preaching, however. In Art. 9, missionary preaching is presumed:

> Before men can come to the liturgy they must be called to faith and conversion.

The same article stresses catechetical preaching which seeks to deepen the faith of the believers.

While the Council does not ignore missionary and catechetical preaching, it is clear that it does center its attention on liturgical preaching or the homily, which liturgical experts describe as a familiar discourse by the pastor with the people, during the liturgical assembly, on biblical texts taken from the liturgy of the day.

Kerygmatic Preaching

Vatican II insisted that a distinctive character permeate the Christian message communicated in the homily: "Its character should be that of a proclamation of God's wonderful works in the history of salvation, that is, the mystery of Christ, which is evermore present and active within us, especially in the celebration of the liturgy" (S.L., Art. 35).

In other words, the document calls for what is known in contemporary homiletics as "kerygmatic" preaching. This use of the term "kerygmatic" preaching does not mean the same as *kerygma* or missionary preaching, the term which Charles H. Dodd has used, and which has been previously quoted. Dodd was attempting to analyze the preaching of the early Church. The three strands of preaching which he discerns have contemporary counterparts, it is true, but the use of "kerygmatic" preaching as a descriptive label today might apply to any of the three traditions identified in the proclamation of the early Christian preachers. Kerygmatic preaching in the contemporary sense, then, would be any preaching which would focus upon the good news of salvation, whether it be *kerygma, paraclesis,* or *didache* preaching in Dodd's sense.

Contemporary kerygmatic preaching received its original impetus in the Roman Catholic Church from liturgical scholars such as J.A. Jungmann in the late 1930's.[8] Its content is the story of salvation as centered in Jesus Christ, who suffered, died, rose from the dead, returned to the Father, now lives in the Spirit of the Church, and will one day return. St. Peter's first sermon after Pentecost (Acts 2:14–39) provides an ideal pattern for kerygmatic preaching in the contemporary sense—a pattern which continued to spread throughout the early Church as is evident in the pages of Acts. The apostles proclaimed the good news of Jesus: that just as God has marvelously acted in the people of Israel, so too has he acted through his Son, Jesus, who by his life and death saved us and continues to save us. This message that "God has acted and continues to act" is essential to the liturgical homily according to Gerard S. Sloyan:

> The worth of the liturgical homily—its indispensable worth—is that it first shows the hearer how God dealt with man in the past so that he can open his heart to His action in the present.[9]

It is important in kerygmatic preaching that the homilist communicate not simply the historical dimension of the Scripture readings but a proclamation of the Christ event as a present reality.

Liturgical Preaching

The articles of *S.L.* and the *Instruction* explain homily in the liturgical sense. The liturgical aspect of the homily is significant for a proper understanding of the renewal of preaching by Vatican II. The Council insisted that the homily is an integral part of the liturgy: "Since the sermon is part of the liturgical service . . ." (*S.L.*, Art. 35); "The homily, therefore, is to be highly esteemed as part of the liturgy itself" (*S.L.*, Art. 52); "For the homily is part of the liturgy of the day" (*Instruction*, Art. 55). Most liturgists today would agree that it is precisely its function in the Mass that distinguishes a homily from other forms of preaching.

The homily is often described as a link or a bridge between the service of the Word and the celebration of the Eucharist. Ancient liturgies manifest a unity between the readings from the Bible and the sacramental action that followed in the Eucharist. The homily functioned as a unifying force; it expounded the Word of God and led to an active and fruitful participation in the Eucharist. This tradition is found in Justin's description of a mid-second century liturgy:

> On the day which is called Sunday we have a common assembly of all who live in the cities or in the outlying dis-

tricts, and the memoirs of the apostles or the writings of the prophets are read, as long as there is time. Then, when the reader has finished, the president of the assembly verbally admonishes and invites all to imitate such examples of virtue. Then we all stand up together and offer up our prayers, and, as we said before, after we finish our prayers, bread and wine and water are presented.[10]

Vatican II restored the ancient tradition of the liturgical homily so "that the intimate connection between words and rites may be apparent in the liturgy" (*S.L.*, Art. 35).

Ancient homilies in the Church contained what theologians call a mystagogical element, i.e., their aim was to introduce the faithful to the mysteries of Christ as celebrated in the Mass. Commenting on the mystagogical characteristic of the homily, John Burke writes:

> While always conscious of the necessity of the initial acts of repentance and conversion the liturgical sermon concentrates on nourishing faith to prepare the worshipers for knowing, active and fruitful participation in the liturgical celebration. It disposes the hearers for sacramental reception which in turn empowers them to live morally and engage in apostolic activity. The liturgical celebration is incomplete without the Word because the mystery of Christ present in the liturgy is manifest only to an active, living faith, and it is only this kind which is fruitful.[11]

Scriptural Preaching

In Art. 35 of *S.L.*, it is indicated that the homily's content should come mainly from scriptural and liturgical sources. Art. 52 of *S.L.* speaks of an expounding from the "sacred text." In the *Instruction* (Art. 54) a definition of the "sacred text" is given: "an explanation either of some aspect of the readings from Holy Scripture or of another text from the Ordinary or Proper of the Mass of the day. . . ."

It has already been noted that modern biblical scholarship profoundly influenced the documents of Vatican II. The

Council insisted that "all the preaching of the Church must be nourished and ruled by Sacred Scripture" (*Divine Revelation,* Art. 21).

When the Council speaks of the scriptural content of the homily, it refers to the readings from the Bible that are assigned to be read for the particular day. Ancient tradition shows that the text of the sacred books read at the liturgy is the first source for the homily which follows.

Frank B. Norris would test whether a homily is authentic by giving a positive answer to the question: "Would a subsequent reading of the pericopes by the faithful be more fruitful and illuminating because of the homily?"[12] The liturgical homily is not a mere exegesis or lecture on the scriptural texts of the day's liturgy, "but a presentation of the text under its spiritual, historical, and pastoral aspects, as being closely related to the spiritual good of the faithful."[13]

The opposite extreme of a homily, which is an exegetical lecture on the literal sense of the scriptural lesson, is a homily, which accommodates the scriptural passages for its own pre-conceived themes. Homileticians and Scripture scholars frequently warn of the dangers of accommodating the Bible, allegorizing it, or using it as a springboard for one's own thoughts. Raymond E. Brown remarks here:

> Preachers may find accommodation easy and may resort to it rather than taking the trouble to investigate the literal sense of Scripture. Occasional use of the imagination in accommodating Scripture can be attractive, but to substitute it for the literal sense is to substitute the man's ingenuity for God's inspired Word.[14]

It should be noted that the *Instruction* (Art. 54) speaks of another source for the homily besides the scriptural readings of the day. Texts from the Ordinary or Proper of the Mass of the day are also mentioned. These texts which are read or sung by the choir, the celebrant and/or the congregation are always biblical in tone.

Art. 35 of *S.L.* states that there are to be more scriptural readings at Mass and that they should be "varied and suitable." Article 51 of the same document states that for "a more representative portion of the Holy Scriptures" to be read to the people, "a set cycle of years" will be required. To implement these directives, a new *Lectionary for Mass* was authorized by Pope Paul VI, April 3, 1969, and became mandatory in the United States on the First Sunday of Advent, November 28, 1971. The compilers of the lectionary sought to present a faithful reflection of the entire Bible. Subsequently, the lectionary was adopted by Presbyterians, Episcopalians, Lutherans, Methodists, the United Church of Christ, and the Disciples of Christ as the basis for the lectionaries that they proposed to their communities. James White, a Methodist liturgical theologian, has described the Roman Catholic lectionary as "Catholicism's greatest gift to Protestant preaching, just as Protestant biblical scholarship has given so much impetus to Catholic preaching."[15]

Relevant Preaching

A final aspect of the character of the homily is its relevance. The *Instruction* (Art. 54) speaks of "the particular needs of the hearers." This phrase is given further elucidation in the advice offered in the *Decree of the Ministry and Life of Priests:*

> If it is to influence the mind of the listener more fruitfully, such preaching must not present God's Word in a general and abstract fashion only, but it must apply the perennial truth of the Gospel to the concrete circumstances of life (Art. 4).

The homily is not a dreamy exposition but a proclamation of God's Word as it relates to the particular circumstances of a specific community living in a specific time in history. Gerard

S. Sloyan offers the following advice for the preacher about to prepare a homily:

> Keep your eye always on the kerygma, the central core of the Gospel that contains in summary the terms of our salvation. Proclaim the meaning of this Gospel of today in relation to it. At the same time, relate your proclamation to this assembly, this feast, these people's lives in Feasterville, Pennsylvania.[16]

In speaking of the mystagogical element of the homily, it was noted that this is not divorced from daily activities of people's lives outside of the liturgical celebration. This is in harmony with Art. 52 of *S.L.* which reads: "By means of the homily the mysteries of the faith and the guiding principles of the Christian life are expounded from the sacred text." In his apostolic exhortation *On Evangelization in the Modern World* Pope Paul VI writes:

> This is why evangelization involves an explicit message, adapted to the different situations constantly being realized, about the rights and duties of every human being, about family life without which personal growth and development is hardly possible, about international life, peace, justice and liberation—a message especially energetic today about liberation.[17]

The homily, therefore, is not simply a message for the time of the liturgical celebration alone, but should seek to influence the personal and social dimensions of our daily Christian life.

Summary

Vatican II introduced a new homiletic approach to the Church's mission by a restoration of the ancient liturgical homily. The word "homily" is now used in the Catholic Church to describe this new kind of preaching which is really a return to the homily of the primitive Church, proclaiming the fact that God has acted and continues to act in our lives. This kerygmatic proclamation arises from the scriptural texts in the liturgy of the day and is addressed to the particular needs of the congregation. An ideal checklist for the new homiletics promoted by the Council includes preaching that is:

1. *Kerygmatic.* The preacher's task is to proclaim the fact that God has acted in history and continues to act in our lives, especially in the person of Jesus Christ who saves us.

2. *Liturgical.* The homily is a link between the liturgy of the Word and the liturgy of the Eucharist. Therefore, the scriptural readings of the Mass of the day are illuminated by the preacher to provide a more intelligent and fruitful celebration of the sacramental action of the Mass. The liturgical homily is a proclamation of *paraclesis,* i.e., it is preached not in the context of a classroom or an evangelical meeting, but to a committed Christian people who come to deepen and celebrate their commitment at the Eucharist.

3. *Scriptural.* The source materials for the preacher's message are the scriptural readings and/or the Ordinary or Proper of the Mass of the day. The homily is not an exegetical lecture on the literal sense of the biblical lesson, nor an accommodation of the lesson for its own pre-conceived themes. It is a pastoral sharing of the text with the people at Mass.

4. *Relevant.* The preacher's message is relevant to the congregation's needs and life situation. An invitation is offered for the people who live in this particular time in history, in this diocese, in this nation, to respond to God's Word not only in the context of the liturgical celebration, but in their daily lives.

II

The Homily and Story

On St. Stephen's Day, the day after Christmas and only a few weeks after his coronation, Pope John XXIII went to visit the prisoners in Rome's Regina Coeli prison. The officials had arranged a special section of the prison where certain well-screened inmates had been brought and the Pope greeted them and gave them his blessing. But he suddenly noticed that there were other prisoners restrained behind bars. "Open the gates," John said. "Don't bar me from them. All of these people are children of the Lord." Then the Pope walked among murderers, thieves, the forgotten, and imprisoned. "You couldn't come to see me," he said, "so I came to see you."

In this one brief story, there is summed up the effect of Pope John's *aggiornamento* on the Church and the world. In this story of an open and pastoral Pope, there is also mirrored God's great love story for us. And what is so refreshing and appealing about John's story is that there is no need to rely on abstract jargon, like "liberation from alienation and oppression." The story tells it in a way that we can begin to grasp God's breaking through in our own stories of fear and imprisonment. And because the story is real, it is powerful. That is why we remember it and will continue to tell it.

Narrative Theology

For more than a decade, some authors have been urging us to return to the story as an authentic mode of theological expression. Sallie TeSelle, for example, speaks of "intermediary theology" which means the various forms of metaphorical language that offer us theological reflection: the story, the poem, the confession.[1] She insists that intermediary theology is not a substitute for systematic theology but a fuller understanding of it. Thus, the *Confessions* of St. Augustine provide us with a theology of grace, but it is a theology that emerges from a confession of his own life experiences of sin and transformation.

Johann Baptist Metz has also contributed to narrative theology by pointing out that "theology is above all concerned with direct experiences expressed in narrative language."[2] Metz argues that Scripture primarily is expressed in story: "from the beginning, the story of creation, to the end, where a vision of the new heaven and the new earth is revealed."[3] He goes on to insist that *logos* (reasoning) is not the original mode of theological expression, but *mythos* (story). While we may express our beliefs in dogmas and creeds, these statements have come from experiences which are initially expressed by some form of narrative.

Christianity itself began as a community of storytellers. The earliest liturgical order has been described simply as: (1) gather the folk, (2) break the bread, and (3) tell the stories. The stories were about Jesus of Nazareth who himself offered such spellbinding stories that they were told and retold by people who found in them a key to their own stories of faith and struggle. The stories of the Bible were always retold in a way that noticed the particular needs and concerns of the listeners. Contact with the original story was not lost, but the new listeners found relevance and renewal in the story retold because it involved them in a personal way. Thus, when Jesus spoke of the shepherd who left everything to search out the lost sheep, he recast an old story from the prophet Ezekiel that the people knew, but now saw in a new light in the person of Jesus and his mission to them.

Investigation of the parables of Jesus by John Dominic Crossan has shown that the parable Jesus preached was not just an imaginative form of rhetoric, but a form of speech congruous with the message of the kingdom itself.[4] The parable, like the kingdom to which Jesus invites us, makes us open to God's surprises. The parable, like our own story, leaves us hanging; it points us to a future promise and direction, but really does not have a last word.

We know, however, that Christianity did not remain a storytelling community. When it entered the Hellenistic world, it inherited *logos* (argument), which for the Greeks was always subordinate to *mythos* (story).

Of course, Christians continued to tell stories. We have a rich heritage that includes the lively tales of the pilgrims on their way to Canterbury, as well as the modern biographies like those of St. Elizabeth Ann Seton. Even philosophers like Pascal and theologians like St. Augustine communicated not only through *logos* but *mythos* as well.

But there was always among theologians a tendency to drive narrative out of the Christian tradition through "demythologization"—and not always without good reason. For example, the Reformers were appalled by many of the sermons of their day which were filled with anecdotes about animals, the Crusades, and exaggerated tales of the saints, but had little to do with the Gospel.

It was unfortunate, however, that in many of the sermons of the early Reformers, story simply was substituted for dry theological argument. The preaching in the Catholic Church following the Council of Trent was no better. Here, too, story often was lost to a colorless exposition of Catholic doctrine which was frequently lifted from the pages of the Roman Catechism.

What narrative theologians are calling for in our day is not a return to story as the only legitimate mode of theological expression. Nor are they demanding a return to simple anecdotes and allegories that will sedate us in our theological struggles. What they are reminding us of is the need to include *mythos* as well as *logos* in our theologizing. Metz believes that "there is a time for storytelling and a time for argument."[5]

Story in Our Time

It seems to many that our time in particular is ripe for a return to storytelling as a form of theological expression. Ours has become a storytelling time mainly for two reasons—*personalism* and the climate of *participation* created by the modern media.

Personalism

We live in a highly personalistic age. It is a time not so much concerned with a conformity to universal principles and rules, but rather with the individual conversion, the personal experience that provides insight to our lives and to our world view. That is why the hot theological issues of our day are so personalistic: abortion, women's ordination, the spiritual rights of minorities, gay people, the divorced, etc.

The horrors of wars and assassinations, the tensions of a technocratic age, the individual quest for freedom and self-determination, the movements toward liberation of oppressed peoples—all these have entered our living rooms via the television set. We live in a global village and so we return to the story again as a way to interpret the events of our lives.

Story is not to be understood here as some fanciful tale. Story in its deepest sense is a quest, a search of this particular person or community in history. Story is the narrative symbol of how we have ordered our experiences with a vision. Urban T. Holmes has described that vision as "a way of seeing in the dark."[6] The story's central character is the pilgrim who in the telling of the story remembers the past in order to understand the present and give meaning to the future. The pilgrim has a story to tell while the wanderer does not. John Navone describes the difference: "The pilgrim differs from the wanderer in that the one has assurance of direction, the other does not. The assurance of direction corresponds to the theological virtue of hope, the spirit with which the pilgrim confronts the wilderness condition."[7] The story contains all those events, dialogues, webs of relationships that make up an individual's or community's search for meaning. When a story is told in an open and honest way, it leads the pilgrim to gratitude and compunction. When stories are shared, often a miracle occurs. F. Scott Fitzgerald once said, "You discover that your longings are universal longings, that you are not lonely and isolated from anyone. You belong. That is part of the beauty of stories."

Thus, psychoanalysis seeks to recover and reinterpret a person's story, especially in the liberation and disclosure of its repressed elements. Sheldon Kopp has described psychoanalysis as "an adventure in narration" where the "basic presumption is that the telling of the tale will itself yield good counsel."[8]

The success of such growth processes as Marriage Encounter and Alcoholics Anonymous depends in large measure in the quality of the telling of the story. Here people begin to share many of their disowned emotions, experiences, dreams, and ideas. Walt Whitman once said of himself, "I am large, I contain a multitude." By sharing stories in a climate of care, people begin to own their stories that contain their many selves and divided hearts. Here we are at the core of the New Testament where the early Church confronted people with their inner divisions so that they might be healed.

The flavor of personalism can be found in the entertainment tastes of our culture. Talk shows abound where guests not only perform but tell us something of their individual stories. Alex Haley's *Roots* which became the most successful production in television history and the popular novels of Elie Wiesel are rooted in real people's stories of struggle and faith.

Participation

It was Marshall McLuhan who first called our attention to the revolutionary impact that the new communications media have had on our lives and our perceptions of the world around us.[9] We do not live in the aural or pre-literate age where speaking was the prime medium of communication.

Nor do we live in the visual or the Gutenberg age where printing was the prime medium of communication. Ours is the electronic age of the telephone, telegraph, television, and the film where all of our senses are massaged at once. Our electronic communications are instantaneous and all pervasive. They have broken down the linear, segmented ways of awareness developed by centuries of reading. A "hot" medium like reading involves a single sense: sight. A "cool" medium like television makes most of our senses participate. In such an age that calls for participation by the listener, the story returns to prominence. Stories do not strike us head-on the way a didactic lesson does, but subtly from behind. They conjure up our own past story and help us to complete the story we are hearing with our own story. In other words, stories invite participation. A prominent storyteller of our day, Robert Béla Wilhelm, has captured the magic of storytelling as an effective aid for participation:

> Human speech always tends toward dialogue, and a speech—or a sermon—is itself an annoying reminder of the one-sided relationship between speaker and audience. The magic of a story is that it casts a spell over us, making us forget that there is a speaker and a topic in front of us. The way this works is very simple: the story takes us out of the room, or hall, or church, and into another world. We forget about his topic, and—perhaps even best of all—we even forget about ourselves.[10]

The Story and the Church

Because the Church is in the world and because our world seems intent on story, it is fitting that story is gaining prominence in the praxis of the Church today.

The charismatic movement has returned the tradition of individual confessions of faith to an almost ritualistic status. The movement of the Holy Spirit is not some vague theological abstraction to charismatics, but as real as the stories they share with one another. People who for so long felt like spectators without the opportunity to participate in the liturgy in a personal way now are able to add their own faith stories to those of the saints.

The impact of narrative theology also has been felt in religious education. At Notre Dame, Elena Malitis developed a course called "Theology as Biography" where the biographies of such people as St. Augustine, Thomas Merton, Dorothy Day, and Martin Luther King, Jr. are read in order to assimilate their metaphors of faith. For example, in reflecting on the metaphors of faith in Dr. King's life—bondage, exodus, promised land—students connect not only with the story of the civil rights leader, but with the biblical story and their own story as well.

The renewed interest in the sharing of the story has found a welcome home in the art of spiritual direction. Spiritual directors today stress the importance of allowing the directee the freedom of knowing his or her story and to experience a journey with the Lord that is always open to surprise and moves toward God's promise. Spiritual direction continues the conversion experience of the biblical theme of vocation, of the Lord who confronts men and women in their own stories, in their own times.

The Story and Preaching

It was only natural that the renewed interest in story today, as reflected in theology, culture, and the praxis of the Church, would soon capture the attention of homileticians. Not that the value of stories was ever dismissed in homiletics. Preaching texts traditionally advocated the use of stories in order to "flesh out" a preacher's ideas. Before Vatican II, one of the most popular series of books that could be spotted in rectories were the stories of Fr. Anthony Tonne. Many preachers effectively told stories in their sermons.

But often the story was misused and underestimated by the preacher, especially in two extremes:

First, the story was not respected as a powerful mode of expression of itself. Too often the story was used as an "ice breaker" or a clever way to warm up or amuse the congregation before getting into the really "serious matter" (usually presented by way of argument). Often there was no connection between the story of the Gospel or feast and the story of the preacher. An example of such preaching went something like this:

> Today we celebrate the feast of the patron saint of our parish, St. Joseph the Worker. St. Joseph was a humble carpenter who with the child Jesus fashioned furniture out of wood. St. Joseph took wood, the gift of God's creation, and recreated that gift for the benefit of all. In our own beautiful church of St. Joseph, we are fortunate to have confessionals that were carved from wood taken from the forest of Bavaria. And so, my dear people, I would like this morning to reflect with you upon three aspects of the new rite of penance.

Second, the story was often manipulated by the preacher who drew out of it and explained more than was there. Here I am speaking of dangerous allegorical interpretation where every detail takes on significance that distracts from the overall meaning and beauty of the story. The preacher values hidden meanings more than the listener's needs. Here the preacher has a field day with the servant who comes to the great wedding banquet without the proper garments (Mt 22:1–14):

> The Mass is the great banquet of our lives. But God, like the king in our Lord's parable, is angry and will punish those who come to Mass and show disrespect to the Blessed Sacrament by wearing shorts or levis. So too will God reject from his love those souls who approach the Mass wearing the dreadful clothes of mortal sin.

Recently, some homileticians have begun to apply insights from biblical studies and narrative theology that have given story a more respectable place in preaching than it had in the past.

1. *The biblical story intersects with our own stories.* Story

is viewed not just as an ornament or clever device to call attention to the message of the biblical lesson. Our stories can often intersect with the biblical story and allow listeners to make the connections. For example, applying a holistic exegesis approach which is directed at both the form *and* content of the Jonah story, Richard A. Jensen suggests:

> The point of what happens in that story is inseparable from the story itself. Preaching need not simply retell the story—although we probably could do just that in some cases. We can, however, create and tell our own stories which elicit responses in the hearer similar to the responses to the original story. What is lost to our hearers so often is the context in which this Jonah story *spoke for itself.* But surely we can tell a story in our own context that speaks for itself and that speaks the story of Jonah anew in our time. That's imaginative recasting. That's preaching as storytelling.[11]

Thus, the goal of the preacher is to meditate on the biblical pericope of the liturgy and ask: How is this story similar to my own story and those of my listeners? What are the feelings, prejudices, values, and particular needs of the people in the biblical story, and in our stories today? What promises, invitations, and hopes are held out to us by the biblical story?

2. *Stories are opportunities for transformation and challenge and not tools for moralizing.* In a culture which places such a high value on personal expression and opinion, it is highly questionable how effective a preacher's moralizing will be. To read into the parable of the man without the proper wedding garment one's own moral bias not only does damage to the original context of the parable, but probably will not be all that persuasive.

The true persuasiveness of stories lies not in their communication of ideas but in a participation of reality. Amos Wilder puts it this way:

> The hearer not only learns about that reality but participates in it. He is invaded by it. Here lies the power and fate-

fulness of art. Jesus' speech had the character, not of instruction of ideas, but of compelling imagination, of spell, of mythical shock and transformation.[12]

Our culture values the courage and example of people whose lives inspire us to a change of heart. That is why we have to keep our eyes and ears open for their stories which are so real and powerful that they do not need allegorization, explanation, or moralizing. We are moved simply in the telling of the tale.

Once in a Palm Sunday homily at Theological College, I tried to highlight the stories of some men and women who were very real to us in that community of Washington, D.C. Their lives seemed to intersect with the humble Jesus who rode into the city of Jerusalem. An excerpt from that homily:

Banquet, Church, Freedom, Community. A promise to be *for* each other. To believe that God is there where people will stay for each other, even for those who do not seem to stay for us.

And we have seen them ride into the city:

Dorothy Day who stays with the poor in the city of New York with a crust of bread and a cup of soup. And there is Banquet.

Cardinal Biayenda who stays in the city of Brazzaville and freely gives his life and ministry to his brothers and sisters. And there is Church.

Martin Luther King, Jr. who stays in the city of Memphis despite bondage, persecution, threats of death. And there is Freedom.

Virginia Mayze and Richie Plavnicks who work beyond their own professional call to feed the poor and shelter battered women at S.O.M.E. and the House of Ruth in this city of Washington. And there is Community.

3. *The story shape of the homily often emerges from the biblical text itself.* Because of our traditional preference of *logos* over *mythos,* we are often tempted not to respect the natural story line of the biblical lesson. We take a parable of Jesus and draw points out of the story and then proceed to explain them. Thus, the story of the prodigal son becomes a discourse with three points corresponding to the prodigal son, the loving Father, and the unforgiving elder son. I once heard of a preacher who spoke of the prodigal son's life as falling into three parts: "his badness, his sadness, and his gladness."

We dress the parable in an Aristotelian straitjacket. We "naturally" see it in three points. We explain everything and thus do not respect the open-endedness of the parable that allows our listeners to participate.

Instead of this logical approach, narrative theologians and some biblical scholars are suggesting that we learn to respect the story line of the Gospel pericope which will provide the narrative shape of our homilies. "That is, the sermon should not be slapped onto a text, extraneous and superfluous to it, but should rather grow out of the text, organic to it, sharing its substance and shape."[13]

In his *Manual on Preaching,* Milton Crum writes that not all sermons need be narrative but "will incorporate some of the dynamic of a story and move like a story."[14] Crum suggests a threefold structure for our preaching: 1. *situation;* 2. *complication;* 3. *resolution.* For example, in Luke's story of the two disciples on the road to Emmaus (Lk 24:13–35) the *situation* is one of encounter with a stranger on the road. Note how, before he preaches, Jesus pays attention to their human situation: "What are you discussing as you go your way?" The *complication* is the disciples' lack of vision—"We were hoping that he was the one who would set Israel free"—and their disbelief in the "astonishing news" in the resurrection. The *resolution* is Jesus' opening up of the story of lost hope in the light of the biblical tradition: "Beginning, then, with Moses and all the prophets, he interpreted for them every passage of Scripture which referred to him."

Once we pay attention to this story line of the Emmaus

tale, we can shape our homily as narrative by beginning with our own *situation* today where God's revelation comes to us in unexpected ways along the road. We can next proceed to our own *complication* where we are often blinded from recognizing the new life that emerges from our death-like experiences. We can then move our story to *resolution* by suggesting how God's story is the only one that allows us to embrace our human stories of fear and despair.

A colleague of Crum's, Scripture scholar Reginald H. Fuller, does point out, however, that while this threefold structure is "profoundly biblical" and can be used to discern the story line of a lesson, we should "not force that pattern on the text, and when it does not have the pattern" we should "take the opportunity to follow a different structure."[15]

4. *A homily contains three stories: the story of the preacher, the story of God, and the story of the listener.* Aristotle is credited with formulating the first verbal communication model. In his *Rhetoric,* he wrote that three elements are basic to any communication: a speaker, a message, and a listener. Homileticians traditionally have applied Aristotle's model to analyze preaching in terms of the preacher, the Gospel message, and the congregation. To this traditional model, there has been added, in recent years, the dimension of story. Teachers of homiletics often describe preaching in terms of the story of the preacher, the story of God, and the story of the listener.

(a) *The Story of the Preacher.* There was a time, not too long ago, when students were instructed to avoid personal references in their homilies. It was considered poor homiletic taste to include a preacher's own stories that could somehow distract from the story of God. While there was some merit in this rubric which restrained navel gazing in the pulpit, it often spared the preacher from any real personal involvement and passion in the story of God. The sermon was considered a message to be delivered, not a story to be shared. But recent developments in pastoral care have stressed the significance of a minister's self-understanding. In order to reach out to others in pastoral care, the minister must first of all be in touch with his or her own story of faith and doubt, love and anger, grace and sorrow. And so, before we dare preach the story of God and presume to know the story of the listener, we must be in touch with our own story, our own search and struggle in the kingdom. In *Biography as Theology,* James McClendon speaks of "metaphors of faith" where a person lives out his or her life under the governance of a vision.[16] Before we attempt to offer a vision of life as proposed in the story of God, or point to the metaphors of faith in the listener's story, we should see our own life as governed by a vision, a story where God's activity can be discerned. I am not speaking here of the preacher whose narcissism distances the listeners, but one who shares something of a personal story of faith in a way that allows people to know that they are included. A culture that values a pesonalistic approach to communication listens to the preacher who dares to be human and vulnerable. Henri Nouwen has written:

> Availability is the primary condition for every dialogue that is to lead to a redemptive insight. A preacher who is not willing to make his understanding of his own faith and doubt, anxiety and hope, fear and joy available as a source of recognition for others can never expect to remove the many obstacles which prevent the Word of God from bearing fruit.[17]

(b) *The Story of God.* A preacher approaches the pulpit with a common story. It is the story of God and his people who are bound together by a special covenant of love, loyalty, and mutual obligation. It is a story in which real people in concrete circumstances are startled, comforted, converted by a God who is a God of grace and commitment in all his promises and fulfillments. While there are millions of stories in the human library of experience and many of them may help us to interpret our world, the story of God as found in the Bible is, for the Christian, *the* story, *the* frame of reference, *the* way of "seeing in the dark." God's story helps us to embrace our own pilgrim stories where he still speaks to us and is there for us. The story of God is not a chronological series of facts and events, but a *kairos* story told by faithful and sinful people who managed to remember what God has said and done for them. We begin our preaching, therefore, not with what we want to say (the story of the preacher) nor necessarily with what the people want to hear (the story of the listener) but with what God has said and continues to say to us. The *Dogmatic Constitution on Divine Revelation* is emphatic here:

> All the preaching of the Church must be nourished and ruled by Sacred Scripture. For in the sacred books, the Father who is in heaven meets his children with great love and speaks with them (Art. 21).

(c) *The Story of the Listener.* As we preach God's story and share our own story, we must also be attentive to the story of the listener. In the 1960's, Reuel L. Howe began to write about the need for dialogical preaching where "preacher and people become partners in the discernment and proclamation by word and action of the Word of God in response to the issues of the day."[18] The concept of dialogical preaching grew out of the dynamics of process theology. The homily was not considered a finished text but a preaching event. The homily was not something communicated from the mind of the preacher to the mind of the listener but something shared between them. The image of story once again proves fitting for an appreciation of dialogical preaching where the story is shared in a partnership that includes God, the preacher, and the listener. If we are not in close contact with the common stories of our congregations, with their particular needs, frustrations, hope and questions, we may eloquently tell God's story and interestingly tell our own, but leave the listeners wondering, "What does all this have to do with me?" In attending to the story of the listener, the preacher should consider seriously what a powerful storyteller, Frederick Buechner, has written:

> Who are they? What is going on inside them? What is happening behind their faces where they have cut themselves

to make them strain to hear the truth if it is told? The preacher must always try to feel what it is like to live inside the skins of the people he is preaching to, to hear the truth as they hear it.[19]

The Three Stories

The homily, therefore, contains three stories of preacher, God, and listener. Obviously, we should avoid a mechanical application of the three story model to each homily we preach. One homily may feature the story of the preacher with more prominence than another which may highlight more the story of God or the story of the listener. What the three story model does provide is a convenient checklist to test whether *to some extent* all three stories are included in a given homily or over a period of time in our preaching. The three story model helps us to discern how we have shared the story of God in a way that mirrors our story and that of our listeners.

Summary

There has emerged in our time a keen interest in story as an authentic form of theological expression. A personalistic age concerned with individual experience and the climate of participation generated by the modern media have welcomed story as a way to view our lives in terms of a journey or a quest. As we share our stories, we remember the past in order to understand the present and give meaning to the future. As we share our common stories, we break from isolation and discover a common vision.

This renewed interest in story as reflected in theology, culture, and the praxis of the Church today has begun to make an impact on our preaching. Stories were often used in preaching in the past, but often the story was not respected as a powerful mode of expression in itself, but as a clever way to warm up the audience before moving into didactic material. Also, the story was often manipulated by the preacher who interpreted its every detail and thus lost the impact of the story.

Insights from biblical studies and narrative theology that can be applied to our preaching include:

1. The biblical story intersects with our own stories.

2. Stories are opportunities for transformation and challenge and not tools for moralizing.

3. The story shape of the homily often emerges from the biblical text itself.

4. The storytelling motif provides a checklist for a homily to determine if it contains the story of the preacher, the story of God, and the story of the listener.

III

The Story of the Preacher

The key to the renewal of the homily by Vatican II is a renewal of the homilist. It is not enough that we understand the kerygmatic, liturgical, scriptural, and relevant dimensions of the homily. It is not enough that we are interesting storytellers. We must also accept, feel deeply, and struggle to practice what we preach Sunday after Sunday. Pope Paul VI put it this way: "Modern man listens more willingly to witnesses than to teachers, and if he does listen to teachers, it is because they are witnesses."[1]

The ancient communication experts Aristotle and Cicero insisted that the character of the speaker was the supreme confirmation or repudiation of what he or she had to say. Ralph Waldo Emerson declared, "What you are speaks so loudly, I cannot hear what you say to the contrary." In judging the effectiveness of the sermons she heard, St. Teresa of Avila laid blame on the preacher's own convictions:

> How is that there are not many who are led by sermons to forsake open sin? Do you know what I think? That it is because preachers have too much worldly wisdom. They are not like the apostles, flinging it all aside and catching fire with love for God; and so their flame gives little heat.[2]

While the character of the preacher has always been significant for the effectiveness of the homily, our age places new demands of honesty and personal involvement upon its preachers. Contemporary homileticians have frequently applied Marshall McLuhan's "The medium is the message" to the importance of the character of the preacher in our age.

Today's theologians have given particular attention to the personal witness of the preacher. Edward Schillebeeckx has written:

> We do not merely toss out dogmas to men who are crying out in dire need. We begin to teach Christian truth successfully by ourselves beginning to live for our fellow men. Our life must itself be the incarnation of what we believe, for only when dogmas are lived do they have any attractive power.[3]

A renewed theology of ministry in the Church views preaching not in terms of performance, but in terms of ministry to God's people. And so I must ask myself, "Do I understand and feel for these people as they too wrestle with God's Word?" "Am I open and human enough to share some of my own wrestling?" "Am I sensitive, caring, uplifting?" "Am I excited about a Person and a Message outside my own powers?" "Does my life give credible witness to my words?" "Am I able to tell some of my own story as I interpret God's story to the people?"

Of course it is always easy to abuse a good thing, even personal involvement in the pulpit. There are some preachers whose personal involvement plunges their homilies into blatant narcissism. There are some preachers who tell their own story of clericalism or anti-clericalism, liberalism or conservatism so well that God's story goes untold. The pulpit has always been, and still is today, an easy platform for self-indulgence, clerical idiosyncrasies and personal hangups that have nothing to do with the Gospel message and people's needs.

St. Paul cautioned those who preached merely their own thing:

> For even if we or an angel from heaven should preach a Gospel not in accord with the one we delivered to you, let a curse be upon him (Gal 1:8).

> I assure you, brothers, the Gospel I proclaimed to you is no mere human invention. I did not receive it from any man, nor was I schooled in it. It came by revelation from Jesus Christ (Gal 1:11–12).

While we must be personally open enough in order to give authenticity and honesty to the homily, it is not our own story that we are called to proclaim, but the story of God. And in this sense, the medium is *not* the message. We are conveyors of a proclamation of God and his Church. The preacher is ordained or delegated to proclaim what the Christian community believes and celebrates: that Jesus died and rose and still breaks through in our lives with his Word in our world today. We are called not to proclaim our own thing, but the kerygma, the good news, the message of salvation.

One of my colleagues, Eugene A. Walsh, suggests that a simple statement of the kerygma might go like this:

> God's faithful covenant love is for all people, no exceptions, no reservations.

> God's covenant love binds us, at one and the same time, in love to God and to all our sisters and brothers.

> God's plan for all people is that they "pass over to the kingdom" by way of love of neighbor. God's plan as revealed by the Spirit of Jesus through creation is the center and focus of all Bible revelation.

> The mission of Jesus is to show God's love to all people, to gather them together and to bring them back to the kingdom.

Jesus carried out his mission through his self-giving in his own life, death and resurrection.

The same mission of Jesus, who is alive and with us to the end of the ages, is carried out now through all people, and in particular by the Church, as charged by Jesus to go out and proclaim the good news.[4]

Of course it is not enough for the preacher simply to repeat the kerygma in twentieth century language. The function of preaching is not merely a kerygma repetition but our personal, faithful, and existential reflection of the good news that we proclaim for the benefit of the community we know and serve. Gene Walsh's statement of the kerygma stems not only from the tradition of the Church, but from a life lived in faith and service to God's people.

For preaching to be authentic, it must involve both the faith of the Church and the preacher's own personal faith. For preaching to be authentic, we must tell our own story of faith, limited and imperfect as it is, in such a way that it illuminates the story of our faithful God and intersects with the story of the community of faith.

Truthful

Hans Küng singles out one feature that best captures the twentieth century—a new passion for truthfulness. In his *Truthfulness: The Future of the Church,*[5] Küng points to many places in our society that cry out for honesty, straightforwardness, genuineness and truthfulness: architecture, which rejects the neo-classic, neo-Gothic, and neo-romantic of another time and demands a style formed by purpose where wood is wood and concrete is concrete; painting, where artists like Matisse do not fear unadulterated color and bold contrasts; novels and poetry and cinema vérité, which attempts to probe the weakness of the individual soul and society with biting honesty; psychology, which gropes to understand people in reality and prevent, as Jung says, the "persona" from masking the true self; philosophy, where Sartre's *authenticité* and Heidegger's *Eigentlichkeit* call men and women away from insincerity and dishonesty; the Church, at Vatican II, a "moment of truth" where the Council began to admit that the Church was in a new world.

Küng defines this modern passion for truthfulness as "more than sincerity or honesty in the narrow sense" but rather "that basic attitude through which individuals or communities, in spite of difficulties, remain true to themselves without dissimulation and without losing their integrity: a genuine candor with oneself, with one's fellow and with God, a genuine candor in thought, word and deed."[6]

In his exhortation *On Evangelization in the Modern World,* Pope Paul VI describes our present century as one that "thirsts for authenticity."[7] He particularly is sensitive to young people who "have a horror of the artificial or false" and "are searching above all for truth and honesty."[8]

Is it any wonder, then, that one of the most stinging and persistent criticisms of modern homilies is their lack of truthfulness? John B. Sheerin has asserted "that the pulpit has lost prestige not because of obsolescent theology or faulty homiletic techniques but because of its dishonesty. By dishonesty I mean not a deliberate distortion of the truth but *clerical passivity,* a lack of honesty in dealing with the messy problems of the day."[9]

Gerard S. Sloyan has called for a new truthfulness in our preaching which is a response to the deep longings of our time and a reflection of the truth of the Gospel:

> Merely speaking the Word is not enough, though. We have done that before—merely speak it. What we need to do is speak the truth and that is by no means easy. It is the truth of ordinary things that needs speaking, not religious truth or *the* truth. If a man should happen to say what is true— however small a fragment of the unequivocally true—God will capitalize the "t". The truth needs neither a semaphore before it nor a red lantern behind. It only needs to be spoken. But that is something very hard to do.[10]

Modern writers have singled out truthfulness as the significant ingredient of their art. We preachers can learn much from such writers as William Faulkner who said that if art is to be relevant to the people of our age, (1) *it must be true:* the creator must feel his or her art with deep persuasion and be able to answer "yes" to the question, "Is it true?"; (2) *it must be loaded with the realities of the human heart:* the artist must delve into the universal and moving questions of love and hate, guilt and forgiveness, pain and joy and hope, life and death.[11]

It is no easy task to risk telling the truth in a post-Watergate age where politicians and Madison Avenue hucksters have forced people to mistrust and wonder about words. In a pain-avoiding society, it takes courage to articulate feelings and events which prefer to remain hidden and covered up.

And so we preachers easily revert to lies—not wicked ones, but shallow ones. We speak in a way that never unmasks our senseless and anxious lives. We prevent God's Word from revealing who we are: weak, sinful, in need of renewal and conversion. We lie by "by saying a few words on the Gospel," which, translated, means repeating the Gospel story that the people have just heard. We lie too by repeating safe dogmatic formulas without any attempt to translate their meaning in a manner that makes sense to people. We fail to make any link between our world and the Word that is proclaimed. We preachers lie by telling people that "God always rewards the good" or "our lives are simple" or explaining "why the vestments today are white." Meanwhile, the violence that is in our streets and in our hearts goes unchallenged; the hunger that is there for real food remains.

Occasionally we preachers are confronted with our "lies" in subtle but dramatic ways. When I was in graduate studies at Temple University, I lived with a community of Christian Brothers at their scholasticate in Elkins Park, Pennsylvania. Each day I would celebrate the liturgy with the brothers and preach a homily. We had a community custom that after the homily a few moments were spent in silence; if one of the brothers wished to add any of his own reflections, he did.

Once, on the Feast of Christ the King, I preached the usual homily one hears on that feast: "Today is the Feast of Christ the King [an exciting and novel introduction] and, as we all know, kings don't mean much to us today. [Really? Ask the fans of Reverend Jim Jones or Elvis.] We live in an age of democratization where kings bother us, etc. But Christ is our King, etc."

The director of the community, Brother David Ryan, said quite simply: "You know, every year on the Feast of Christ the King, we usually hear this same homily: [Kings don't mean much to us today. We live in an age of democratization where kings bother us, etc.]. But the truth is, right here in this community our problem seems to be the fact that each of us wants to be king over one another, but Jesus is telling us something different."

I remained seated, pondering David's wisdom. He had preached the real homily that day in a few simple sentences because he spoke the truth. He was not afraid to give a name to our sinfulness, nor was he shy to point to Christ's new way. David did not flinch to speak the sad news, to name it for what it was, before he spoke the good news.

An exercise for truthful preaching that I have found valuable in my own homily preparation, and one which I often suggest to my students, is to read aloud one of your homilies and, after each line, pause for a few seconds to ask yourself some challenging questions: Do I believe this? Is what I say evident in my life and in the lives of the people I know? How strongly can I say "yes" to this sentence? If you hear yourself mumbling lukewarm responses, you can bet that your congregation will react in the same way. If you can honestly own the lines of your homily, most probably your listeners will own them as well.

Human

I always begin my first class in *Introduction to Preaching* by asking the students why they want to preach. The answers I hear always renew my hope in today's ministers: "I want to preach the Gospel in a way that will change lives." "I don't want to bore people or turn them off, as I have been." "I want to share the Lord as I have experienced him, and I believe that one of the most effective places to do that is in the pulpit."

But what happens to us preachers over the years that causes us to lose this zeal for sharing God's Word? Why does preaching take such a low priority in our work effort? Why do we reach for the canned homily while watching television on Saturday night? Why do we stop preaching the Word in a truthful way?

No preacher sets out to be a mechanical speaker, a deliberate hypocrite, a lazy apostle. I think what we often forget, however, is who we are. St. Paul reminded his congregation in Lycaonia who he and Barnabas were as preachers. "We are only men, human like you. We are bringing you the good news that will convert you from just such follies as these to the living God, 'the one who made heaven and earth and the sea and all that is in them' " (Acts 14:15). We are human like you. In other words, like the people to whom we preach, we have needs and doubts. Like our listeners, we too pass through various stages in life's journey. Like our congregation, we are weak and sinful, especially when the internal and external pressures of personal and ministerial life force us to compromise what is in our hearts. Without the aid of a friend, advisor, spiritual director, guru—however you name that special person—with whom we can be truthful and open, with whom we can feel God's finger in our lives, with whom we can make free human choices, we soon forget that "we are human like you."

When we are not in touch with our humanity, we soon begin to fake the part, learn the lines, and make the right moves since the show must go on. When we are not in touch with our humanity, we begin to trust our own clever devices or the canned words of some homiletic wizard rather than the Lord whose grace is enough for us and whose power reaches perfection in our weakness (2 Cor 12:9). When we are not in touch with our humanity, we stop praying, trusting, caring. That is when we begin to preach what is not truthful and human.

I am not speaking here of preachers who speak their own story so loudly that God's story and the story of the listener go untold. That is a danger. I remember a priest in my home town whose perpetual homiletic metaphors were his visits to Europe. Since most of his parishioners could never afford a trip abroad, their pastor's homilies became real ego-trips. There was little they could relate to, and so they walked away thinking, "That was nice, but what did it have to do with God or me?" I was confronted once by a parishioner who liked my analysis of current films but suggested that my homilies were being dubbed "Sunday Morning at the Movies" by some in the congregation. My own story of love for films was overshadowing the story of my listeners and the good news.

The pulpit can be a convenient niche for narcissism, for working out clerical problems of authority or loneliness, for masking our anger and prejudices, and for parading our wit and theological talents. This is an abuse of the preacher's story and must always be checked by a few friends in our congregations who can give us healthy critiques.

When I speak of the need for us preachers to share our humanity, I am suggesting an honest confessing of our sins, doubts, and struggles as well as our faith. Myron R. Chartier stresses the importance of this human sharing:

> The preacher's task is to make God visible through the transparency of his or her own person. When the preacher tries to be something other than he or she is, then the good news of the Gospel is blocked by deception. The truth of the incarnation is that God has been revealed in humanity. To the degree that the preacher can be authentically human by revealing self, he or she is in the position to be an instrument of the revelation of God. Appropriate self-disclosure on the part of the preacher provides the congregation a point of identification with the Word.[12]

We can apply Henri Nouwen's haunting metaphor of the "wounded healer" to our preaching of the Word. Nouwen speaks of the minister who heals not from strength but from defeat:

> For the minister is called to recognize the sufferings of his time in his own heart and make that recognition the starting point of his service. Whether he tries to enter into a dislocated world, relate to a convulsive generation, or speak to a dying man, his service will not be perceived as authentic unless it comes from a heart wounded by the suffering about which he speaks.[13]

A "wounded healer" preacher is not a gloomy one. We must learn how to laugh at ourselves in the pulpit. Pope John Paul II, preaching to his people on a 90° Polish summer day, was human enough to say, "Rome was too hot, so I came to Poland for some cool weather. You see, even the Pope makes mistakes." The crowds roared.

When we can chuckle at our own foibles as we tell our story, our fellow pilgrims will chuckle, too, at their own. They will turn the phrase around and say, "Preacher, you are only a human being like me." When that wonderful moment of identification occurs, you can be sure that the good news has a real chance of being heard and believed.

Insightful

There is no more devastating response to a homily than a "so what?" In the telling of our story, we have missed the link between human reality and the good news. We have made religion a kind of appendix to our story rather than letting it leap out of its every chapter. In a word, we have failed to offer any insight into our lives. Our homily sounds like this:

> The church begins again the great season of Advent. The Church dons its purple in hushed preparation of the wondrous Christ event that we will celebrate at Christmas and in joyful anticipation of the even more wondrous eschatological reality of Christ in our lives. And, thus, it is that we

listen to the Gospel today about the destruction of the temple in Jerusalem.

A listener, hearing such a spooky homily, might rightfully respond, "So what? What does this have to do with my life, my fears, my needs? And please don't tell me that I shouldn't be commercial at this season of the year. You said the same thing last year. And besides, I saw you rushing through the mall the other night and I could tell you were frustrated too. You're talking about the destruction of the temple and I'm worrying about the destruction of my savings account!"

Jesus preached in a way that gave insight into his followers' lives. He began with the common occurrences of people and dared to invite them to dig deeply into the ordinary in order to experience the finger of God. He invited people to interpret the signs of the times, even when those signs were as tiny as mustard seeds.

Jesus' preaching began with real events and real questions, not time-honored truths. What he did was use all the religious traditions of his people to give insight into the events of people's lives. Jesus didn't look "out there" for his homilies, but inside people's lives, inside his world, inside his own life and mission which he pondered on lonely, desert nights. That is why nothing escaped his attention: a pesty woman's story shed light on prayer and the persistence of God's kingdom; a rich young man who wanted to hold on, shed light on the cost of being a disciple; a runt in a tree shed light on the first mission of life—hospitality.

The parables he preached have been called "real slices of life." Remember "Godspell" where we applauded, laughed, wept, when we saw the parables in the limelight? The parables are human, funny, tragic; they cannot be denied or put aside because they are real and are still happening in our lives.

Bill Cosby calls his brand of humor "uh-huh" humor because he talks about real events in people's lives. Of course, his jokes emerge from his own story of a poor black kid growing up in North Philadelphia and playing football for Temple when they always lost. But Cosby tells his story in such a way that it mirrors our own. It is real and so we laugh and say, "Uh-huh, that's the way it is!" I am not suggesting we preachers become stand-up comics, but I think we can learn a lot from Cosby's "uh-huh" way of telling a story.

A few years ago my Uncle John died. He was a strong, quiet, faithful man who left a deep impression on his kin. In his funeral homily, I did not have to point to his Christian virtues; we knew them. What I tried to do was to see Uncle John's life through the Gospel. I talked about the ordinary events of his life and how they touched us. Afterward, a cousin of mine said, "Thank you for what you said today. You know, it all finally made sense to me." She was telling me it was an "uh-huh" homily. Thank God, my story shed light on hers. Henri Nouwen speaks of this moment of homiletic insight when he shares a listener's response:

> What you say loudly, I whispered in the dark; what you pronounce so clearly, I had some suspicion about; what you put in the foreground, I felt in the back of my mind; what you hold so firmly in your hand always slipped through my fingers. Yes, I find myself in your words because your words come from the depths of human experiences and, therefore, are not just yours but also mine, and your insights do not just belong to you, but are mine as well.[14]

Interpretive

During the 1974 Synod of Bishops in Rome on evangelization, there was a serious dialogue about the role of preaching in the post-Vatican II Church. Some bishops urged a three-year cycle of homilies, based on the Scripture readings, but focused on the presentation of the Catholic faith. The Church took a similar catechetical approach to preaching during the Counter-Reformation. There were other bishops at the Synod, however, who questioned a return to the catechetical homily. One bishop summed up their position well when he said: "What is needed now in our world and Church is not an explanation of God but an experience of God."

Experience is the key to telling our story in a truthful, human, and insightful way. We interpret life because we have experienced it. We are not merely conveyors of ideas, but proclaimers of God in our lives. We have been touched by the Gospel in our own life of faith and struggle. Robert Frost once said: "Every poem begins with a lump in the throat." The same should be said of every homily.

In his homiletic classic *Design for Preaching*,[15] H. Grady Davis suggests that there are three processes we preachers must attend to while seeking to share our experiences and give an interpretation to our lives: (1) *diagnosis,* where we ask: What have we? (2) *etiology,* where we ask: How come? (3) *prescription,* where we suggest what to do.

Diagnosis is the process where we observe, where we talk about the way things are, give our world viewpoint. It is the process of the novelist, the poet, the musician, the playwright, the sculptor who produces his or her art to help interpret our lives, to say, "This is the way it is."

Etiology is the process which advances causes for why we are the way we are. It is the process of the historian, the therapist, the scientist who seeks to isolate the independent variable in order to interpret our lives and tell us: "This is why we are who we are."

Prescription is the process of the physician who has observed how we are and why we are this way and then suggests a remedy, a medicine, a plan for the future.

When someone says "Don't preach to me," he or she is referring to the prescriptive process of interpretation. Often our preaching is too identified with the prescriptive and misses the diagnostic and etiological aspects. It is easy for the preacher to fall into the prescriptive mode: "Let us take this time-honored truth and apply it to our lives today and we will be happy and rewarded; if we don't, we will be punished." Some have called such a homily a "salad sermon" since it is so full of "let us."

We cannot ignore the prescriptive; we must not fear our prophetic role of challenge. Jesus did not shrink from telling the people: "Love your enemies; leave all and follow me; carry your cross daily." But his prescriptions were supported by his diagnosis of the situation. How often his friends and enemies pose questions to him: "What are we to do?" "How can we feed all these people with a few loaves and a couple of fish?" "Should we pay tribute to Caesar or not?" "Who is my neighbor?" But he always turns the tables and tells them first who they are, what their lives are all about.

They drag the town whore to his feet and shout, "What are we to do with her? The Law says she should be stoned." But Jesus does not rush to prescription. He looks at the men gripping their stones. He looks into the bloodshot eyes of the painted girl shaking at his feet. And then he stoops to doodle in the sand the way we preachers must doodle on our pads as we think about what is happening. He is observing, and when he says, "He who is without sin should be the first to cast a stone," Jesus is telling them who they are: sinners, compromisers, hypocrites. He is interpreting their lives, and as they walk away, they drop their stones, and if you listen closely you can hear their faint "uh-huhs." Then he turns to her and dares the prescriptive: "Go, sin no more!"

A fruitful exercise for us preachers is to read all of the homilies we have preached after a year's time, asking the questions: "What interpretation of life have I shared with the people?" "Is my story gloomy, cynical, hopeful, joyful, overly idealistic, clerical, iconoclastic?" "Do I paint a black and white picture of reality or do I dare shed light on the shades of gray?" This exercise can help us see how much our story is helping or hindering the story of God and the story of the listener from being heard.

Summary

The preacher is called to proclaim "the Gospel once delivered to the saints." The preacher tells again the wonderful story of how God has always been with and for his people and how the good news still breaks through in our lives today, even in the midst of news that is very bad.

But in the telling of the story of God, we preachers cannot

help but tell our own story of faith, weak and imperfect as it is. "The medium is the message." God's Word is spoken through human words which emerge from the preacher's own story.

Reflecting on the story of the preacher in a homily, we can turn to the following checklist:

1. *Truthful:* The preacher dares to tell it like it is. We speak our story in a way that responds to our modern world's passion for truthfulness. We avoid the shallow lies that never unmask our senseless and anxious lives. We can say "yes" to our homily because that is how we have experienced life and the Gospel.

2. *Human:* We must not fear our own humanity. We tell our story as a fellow pilgrim who is not afraid to reveal doubt as well as faith. We speak not only from our victories, but also from our defeats. We are "wounded healers" who are able to laugh at ourselves even in the pulpit.

3. *Insightful:* In the telling of our story, we shed light on God's story and mirror the stories of our listeners. We talk about life as we know it and have experienced it. We are able to show people that faith is not in the clouds, but in our hands, in the real events of our lives. Our listeners say "uh-huh" to our story because it has told them something about their own that matters.

4. *Interpretive:* The preacher is like the poet who dares to tell us what life is all about, why it is so and what we should do about it. We are careful about attributing simplistic causes and motives to our lives. And before we tell our listeners what to do, we tell them who we are and what is happening right now in our lives.

IV

The Story of God

A popular book when I was in the seminary was Malcolm Boyd's *Are You Running With Me, Jesus?* Its popularity mirrored the personal quest for freedom and meaning ushered in by the turbulent 1960's. Its title reflected a special attention to the private stories of pilgrims on the way. In the late 1970's, however, Boyd wrote another book whose title suggested that a more balanced approach to the dialogue between the individual and God was emerging: *Am I Running With You, God?* While the story of the individual pilgrim is basic for authentic spirituality and biblical faith, a number of current authors are reminding us that our faith quest does not begin nor end with the pilgrim's story, but with the story of God.

One such author is biblical scholar James Sanders. Sanders does not deny the precious importance of our private stories of faith, but declares: "God has a story too; and it is his story which is our real purpose in being. It is God's story in Torah and in Christ which is Gospel for the Christian."[1] It is God's story that provides us the way of "seeing in the dark." It is God's story, as we find in the Bible, that, far from denying our individual stories of faith, always invites us to embrace our stories as they are, imperfect and puzzling, yet filled with the possibility of conversion, liberation, and new life.

In Chapter I, we saw how preachers during various periods of the history of the Church substituted the story of God with stories that suited their own goals. The pulpit often became a platform for Scholastic debates, denunciations of heresies, the stories of saints and, especially, during the period between Trent and Vatican II, a catechetical spot for the explanation of doctrinal topics that were often totally unrelated to the Scripture readings of the liturgy. When Scripture was quoted, it was often used to accommodate a preacher's own topic or to "prove" some point of argumentation.

Vatican II's renewal of the ancient homily signaled a return to the proclamation of the story of God: "All the preaching of the Church must be nourished and ruled by Sacred Scripture" (*Constitution on Divine Revelation,* Art. 21). The character of the homily "should be that of a proclamation of God's wonderful works in the history of salvation" (*S.L.,* Art. 35).

The Lectionary

The *Constitution on the Sacred Liturgy* directed that "the treasures of the Bible are to be opened up more lavishly so that a richer fare may be provided for the faithful at the table of God's Word" (Art. 51). From this directive came the *Lectionary for Mass* (1969) compiled by some thirty biblical scholars to give worshipers a feel for the whole of God's story.

The tradition of planning a set of readings from Scripture has its roots in ancient Jewish synagogue ritual when the Torah was read as a first reading and the prophets as a second reading at the dismissal part of the service. There are some biblical scholars who believe that the Gospels themselves reveal a series of liturgical pericopes. As early as the fourth century in *The Apostolic Constitutions,* there is reference to "reading of the law and the prophets of our epistles and the Acts, as well as the Gospels," a five-lesson sequence (8.5.5; cf. 2.57.5).

Lectionaries provide preachers with an orderly succession of Scripture readings which reflect the liturgical calendar of the worshiping community. Preachers need not search for their own homiletic schemes. A lectionary challenges "the subjectivity of one local preacher wondering what to read for the next week, and its predetermined scope allows what otherwise might be avoided to come up naturally."[2]

Purpose

The designers of the lectionary selected the Scripture readings to fit the liturgical calendar of the Church. The liturgical calendar developed quite naturally "because humans are creatures of time and space, and they need time and space in order to take hold of any great truth or reality and to make it their own."[3] The great truth we celebrate year after year is the mystery of Christ, which is ever made present and active within us, especially in the celebration of the liturgy" (*S.L.,* Art. 35). The lectionary is predominantly Christological. The purpose of the lectionary is to proclaim the dying and rising of Christ made present in us through faith and baptism. Thus, the story of God expressed in Jesus becomes our story as well.

William Skudlarek's intelligent new book on liturgical preaching reminds us:

> The lectionary was not to be ordered around a "history of salvation" motif (understood as a line running from the creation to the second coming), or around a systematic presentation of the theological teachings of the Church, or according to a literary analysis of the parts of the Bible that were to be used. Nor were the readings to be chosen and ordered for the primary purpose of exhorting and encouraging people to lead more Christian lives.[4]

Skudlarek's reminder needs to be highlighted, especially since some recent authors of homiletic books and aids are attempting to present the doctrinal and ethical teachings of the Church by way of a three year cycle of readings in the lectionary. Obviously, there is a pressing need to present these teachings, but to force them out of the readings of the lectionary not only does damage to the primary purpose of the lectionary, but twists God's story to suit our own. One can concede that such a catechetical plan might be possible if an author ignores the main point of the readings on a particular Sunday and uses some minor point as the springboard for a topical sermon. One can also understand the temptation to turn the Sunday congregation into a class since it is the one time when there is a large assembly of believers present. But the church is not a classroom.

Besides, why do we think that explaining things (information) is more pressing than offering a new way of looking at our lives and our world (formation)? What the anguished Kierkegaard noted in his own time applies to ours as well: "There is no lack of information in a Christian land; something else is lacking."[5] Learning theorists today, like Malcolm Knowles, insist that an adult will not absorb any information that he or she does not in some felt way have a need to absorb.

I suspect that the tendency to offer information rather than invite formation is really an easy way out of the ongoing wrestling with God's story that challenges our lives and our world. God's story is a two-edged sword. "The readings of the Bible can offer to us ways of understanding our life which are quite different from our own ways and perhaps even in contradiction."[6]

I am convinced that if we preachers take seriously the purpose of the lectionary, which is to proclaim the dying and rising of Christ and to discern and celebrate this same passover in our own lives and world, a meaning would be given to people who are hungry for good news. Then adult religious education programs, which are biblically oriented, would naturally follow.

To exegete, interpret, and brood over the Scriptures requires work, faith, and imagination. Such preaching involves not just information about God, but an invitation to experience God in our lives and in our world. Such preaching demands respect for God's story, sensitivity to the listeners' story, and the risky business of embracing our own stories.

Plan

The choice and arrangement of the lectionary readings are governed by principles which are explained in the "Introduction to the Lectionary":

> In arranging the texts the purpose was to assign those of greatest importance to Sundays and feasts when the Christian people are bound to celebrate the Eucharist together. In this way the faithful will be able to hear the principal portions of God's revealed Word over a suitable period of time. Other biblical readings which to some degree complement these texts are arranged in a separate series for weekdays.[7]

Sunday and feast days always have three lessons, the first taken from the Old Testament (its place is substituted by Acts in Eastertide), the second from the epistles (or Revelation) and the third from the Gospels. For most of the year, the Gospel pericopes are semi-continuous from a book in its chapter sequence. The Old Testament readings do not manifest any such sequence. They are selected to provide background, to reinforce or to provide contrast to the Gospel of the day. The epistle selections are read semi-continuously in certain seasons, in blocks of three to sixteen weeks. The epistle reading was not selected to relate to the main point of the Gospel and Old Testament readings, but has its own sequence from week to week. Thus, except for the seasons of Advent, Lent, Eastertide, and the principal feasts, the three lessons do not evidence a unity of theme.

The essential characteristic which differentiates each year from another is the Gospel which is read as the principal lesson: Year A, Matthew; Year B, Mark; Year C, Luke. Because Mark is shorter than the other Synoptics, it is complemented with readings from John. The Fourth Gospel is allotted its traditional privileged position throughout the cycle, i.e., it is read on several important feasts, in Lent and Eastertide.

Although the Gospel pericope provides a homiletic theme so too do the semi-continuous readings of each year offer a general homiletic theme from one Sunday to another. For example, from the Fifteenth to the Twenty-First Sunday of the Year, Year B, the Epistle to the Ephesians is read. General themes are also grouped together throughout a liturgical season. For example, all the Sundays of Advent refer to different aspects of the coming of the Lord; from Easter Sunday until the Third Sunday of Easter, the Gospel recounts the appearance of the Lord.

In summary:

1. The plan of the lectionary encourages the preacher to concentrate on the Gospel for the main thrust of the homily.

2. The Old Testament reading should provide the proper harmonization and context for the Gospel lesson.

3. The second lesson has its own sequence and, except for primary feasts and the seasons of Advent, Lent and Eastertide, does not harmonize with the Old Testament and Gospel readings.

Problems

Although some liturgists consider the lectionary to be the most carefully prepared in the history of the Church, many others point to its flaws which present practical problems for the preacher.

1. *Devaluation of the Old Testament.* Since the Gospel lesson sets the theme for the liturgical calendar, the choice of the Old Testament reading was made solely for the purpose of harmonization. This could allow some preachers to continue a hermeneutic of evolutionism—the anti-Semitic hermeneutic that what is later Bible is somehow better. Contemporary scholars in intertestamental studies point to the inadequacy of the assumption that the Old Testament is "fulfilled" in the New Testament. These biblical scholars show how New Testa-

ment authors often modified and wove Old Testament traditions into the New Testament for their own hermeneutical reasons. Gerard Sloyan cautions against the fulfillment principle of interpretation where Jews emerge incomplete, disloyal, and condemned, while the disciples in the New Testament are justified in Jesus:

> It might be called "realized eschatology with a vengeance." This is the triumphal understanding that all that has been realized in the Christ of glory has been realized in Christians. Since lectionary choices can contribute to this mentality, it must be all the more vigilantly resisted when they are employed.[8]

As a corrective to this misuse of the harmonization between the Old Testament and Gospel readings from the lectionary, Sloyan advises the use of the "oldest principle of biblical interpretation. It is that later verbal symbols throw light on earlier ones in a cascade of imagery that conveys some sense of the divine."[9] Thus, instead of reading into the Old Testament and the Gospel lessons a fulfillment principle of history, the preacher uses a hermeneutic which seeks to discern the visible symbols of an unseen God.

Because the Old Testament readings were selected to harmonize with the Gospel lessons, many of the great themes in which God dealt and continues to deal with his people are absent. The theme of God's grandeur of creation is read only at the Easter Vigil when few people are present; the lectionary does not highlight the wretchedness of human life found in Job or in the Psalms; the great moral tales (e.g., the story of David's relationship with Nabal and Abigail) which help the hearer wrestle with human dilemmas are often ignored and substituted for exhortations to virtue such as those found in the Book of Proverbs.

Liberation theologians operating with their "hermeneutic of suspicion" are critical of the fact that much of the struggle between the powerful and the powerless from the Old Testament is missing in the lectionary.[10] For example, while there are many selections from Deuteronomy and Leviticus, the more radical views of these two books are not presented: that the land belongs to God and cannot be held forever by anyone. The sole text from Micah for the Fourth Sunday of Advent (Year C) is chosen because of its reference to Bethlehem as the birthplace of the ruler of Israel. This brief text does not allow the prophet's message of a new order of peace and justice to be proclaimed.

Once again, Gerard Sloyan notes this problem area in the lectionary and offers homiletic advice:

> What needs to be explored, then, is the great themes of the Israelite and Christian religions that are featured aside from the central one of God's faithfulness to his promises in Jesus Christ.[11]

2. *The Second Reading.* Since the second reading on an ordinary Sunday of the Church year is not meant to harmonize with the Old Testament and Gospel lessons, it does cause problems for hearers and preachers of God's Word. It is similar to an orchestra beginning with an overture to *Romeo and Juliet* (Old Testament reading), then switching to the music of *Oklahoma* (second reading), and finally ending with the music of *West Side Story* (Gospel reading). One could see the connection between *Romeo and Juliet* and *West Side Story,* but *Oklahoma* in the middle of the common theme of star-crossed lovers is confusing and out of place. However, this does not prevent some preachers and authors of homiletic services and doctrinal series on the readings of the lectionary from finding a common theme throughout all three readings for every Sunday of the Church year. In forcing a common theme on all three readings, they often miss the major theme of one or more of the readings and, "with considerable ingenuity, find a strained connection by means of minor emphasis or incidentals."[12]

Some compilers of the lectionary wanted only two readings (Old Testament and Gospel) but, because of the desire to include most of the Bible in the liturgy, the second lesson was added. In a future revision of the lectionary, some liturgists propose that the letter be read at the end of the liturgy as a dismissal reading, similar to the *haftara* in the ancient Jewish synagogue service.

In the meantime, I find William Skudlarek's suggestion on how the preacher should use the second reading in homiletic preparation to be a sound one:

> Thus as you work with the Gospel, and with the Old Testament lesson that corresponds to it, keep your eye on the epistle. Let it be there, on the horizon, in the background, lurking, as it were, in the shadows. As you read it—and multiple readings are absolutely necessary—in connection with the other texts, do not force it to relate to the Gospel and Old Testament lesson. Simply let yourself be open to the ways in which this lesson can draw further meaning from the text of the Gospel, can throw light on it, can be seen as indicating a way in which the paschal mystery in Christ is being completed, or needs to be completed, in us.[13]

It should be noted here that the homilist does have a choice of preaching on the great themes of the Gospel with the Old Testament reading as background or of preaching a series of homilies from the semi-continuous cycle of the epistle lessons. I stress *series* of homilies, since it would not be in harmony with the purpose of the lectionary and the liturgical year to skip from Gospel to epistle from Sunday to Sunday.

3. *Special Themes.* While the obvious advantages to the lectionary are uniformity, harmony with the liturgical year, and a challenge to the subjectivity of the local preacher or congregation, it must also be admitted that following a set pattern of Scripture readings is sometimes restrictive. It is especially so when certain memorials such as Mother's Day, Fourth of July, Vocation Sunday, Mission Sunday, etc., or local and national events do not mirror the themes of God's story for that particular liturgy. In such cases, pastoral prudence and flexibility are important.

First of all, prudence is essential because we should be slow to substitute our own stories for the story of God as it unfolds in the liturgical year. Vatican II's renewal of the liturgy sought to restore the paschal mystery of Christ that had often been overshadowed by minor themes and festivals. Historically, we know that the pulpit has been a convenient place to promote and announce events and causes that had little to do with the Bible. Some liturgists have noticed a new encroachment on the Sunday readings coming from chancery offices promoting various theme Sundays or suggesting the reading of a letter from the local ordinary in place of the homily. While a bishop has a right and a duty to teach his people, such letters and themes should be brief and few in number, and, when they are necessary, should reflect the major themes of the Sunday Scripture readings. Otherwise, we do great damage to the integrity of the liturgy of the Word by proclaiming readings that set up one major theme and then proceed to preach on another.

Secondly, we can be flexible with the lectionary. Obviously, there will be times when great events cannot be ignored by the preacher since they reflect, in the Council's words, "the concrete circumstances of life." When they do occur, and if, after careful meditating on the Scripture readings of the day, the Scripture themes still do not seem to match our particular concerns, we should choose readings from Scripture that do. A case can be made on this principle of flexibility from the *General Instruction on the Order of Mass* even though it does refer to the weekday readings: "A priest may choose from the readings of that week those most suitable for the group" (#319).

Interpreting God's Story

The power of the story retold is dramatically captured by Martin Buber's Hasidic tale:

> My grandfather was lame. Once he was asked to tell a story about his teacher and he told how the Holy Baal Shem Tov used to jump and dance when he was praying. My grandfather stood up while he was telling the story and the story

carried him away so much that he had to jump and dance to show how the master had done it. From that moment, he was healed. This is how stories ought to be told.[14]

The miracle of good storytelling is that tellers and listeners are healed because they recognize the story as their own. Preaching God's story that way begins with the very manner in which the Scriptures are proclaimed. The preacher points to the book or the preacher's face is covered by the lectionary while announcing "This is the Gospel of the Lord." There is little eye contact and no real dialogue between preacher and listeners. What does this body language say about the Bible as the Word of God and about the preacher's active faith in God's Word as spoken to us now? The impression is given that the text of the Bible is the Word of God alone. Such preachers approach the Bible as an ancient treasure chest where gems of wisdom are examined and then applied to the human situation now. In this approach, we seek to discover how God acted in the past (usually presented in a neat package of Divine Providence) and then scratch our heads and try to apply this same story of God to our own times. Preachers seek to explain the obscure, confusing ancient stories of the Bible so that their morals can be applied to our stories today.

But there is another way to interpret the story of God. It is found in the Hebrew verb *dabar* which indicates word, not as a static symbol, but word spoken as an action, an event. "Word of God, according to biblical tradition, thus seeks to be understood as a word event that does not go out of date but constantly renews itself, does not create closed areas of special interest but opens up the world, does not enforce uniformity but is linguistically creative."[15] Here, the preachers, like the grandfather in our Hasidic tale, are carried away by the ancient story until it becomes our own. Here the Bible becomes God's Word when it is proclaimed to give meaning to a believing individual or community. Bernard Cooke states it this way, "Somehow human experience and Bible together form 'word of God.' "[16] The preacher does not approach the Bible as some obscure piece of ancient literature that needs to be explained and then applied to our lives. It is rather that our lives are obscure and unintelligible and need to be interpreted by the Bible. Gerhard Ebeling and Ernst Fuchs have reminded us that the Word of God is not interpreted; it interprets. What needs to be interpreted, then, is our lives in the light of God's story.

Hermeneutics, the science of interpreting Scripture, involves both an *exegesis* of the text to discover what it *meant* in the original and a *transposition* of that text to what it means for our own context. In homiletics, it is the process of seeing the *now* in terms of the *then*.

Now and Then

This past Good Friday, I watched the stations of the cross on the six o'clock TV news. The priests and parishioners of Sts. Paul and Augustine Church in Washington, D.C. did not make the stations in the traditional way of staying in the church building. Instead, they took to the streets and gave witness to the *via dolorosa* of the nation's capital. There they united the story of Christ's struggle and crucifixion to the contemporary "stations" of street crime and violence, corners of prostitution, shelters for battered women and the hungry. The story was the same, but it shed new light on our lives today.

Taking God's story to the streets illustrates the two poles of biblical preaching that are always in tension, the *then* of the ancient biblical story and the *now* of our own story. The word "tension" is crucial because dangerous theological traps occur when preachers succumb to exaggerating either the *then* or the *now*. The first results in *biblicism,* a fascination with the text, but a devaluation of the present moment of grace. The second extreme results in *eisegesis,* a fixation on the present moment while using the text as a springboard to support one's own concerns and bias.

The preacher involved in *biblicism* is more comfortable in quoting chapter and verse than reading the signs of the times.

This is the preacher who tells us, "Let us return to ancient Jerusalem for a few minutes this morning." Details are given of the ancient culture and story of the Bible that would be more appropriate for a class than a worshiping community. Footnotes are provided from scriptural commentaries; gems of wisdom are extracted from the Gospel; "points" are drawn out of the story and perhaps a feeble attempt is made to apply them to our lives. The impression is given that God's revelation ended with the last book of the Bible. God's story is told, but ours is neglected.

On the other hand, the preacher involved in *eisegesis* is more concerned with contemporary needs or a particular theological bias than the accumulated revelation of how and why God acted in the biblical story. Eisegesis is not concerned with drawing God's story out of the text, but reading our story into it. Since the Bible spans five ancient eras and covers a wide gamut of human problems and events, it is pluralistic enough to provide the preacher with a wealth of images, ideas and emotions. If we are myopically concerned with our own story or the story of the listener, we can use the pluralistic nature of God's story as a springboard for supporting our own concerns and biases. Carl Sandburg once told the story of a group of applicants for a job who were asked only one question by the interviewer: "How much is two plus two?" All the applicants responded "Four," except for the one who was hired. That person answered, "It amounts to whatever you want it to, sir." DeWitte Holland's *Sermons in American History* clearly demonstrates how preachers, both conservative and liberal, often manipulated the Bible to mean only what they wanted it to mean. A preacher whose gaze is only on the present moment leaves the impression that God's revelation begins and ends with us. Because our view of the way things are is central, God's story, which often contradicts our view, is neglected.

It is impossible to return to ancient Jerusalem or pretend we are first century Christians. We are not. It is blasphemous to theologize only with our own story, ignoring the fact that "God has a story too." A preacher can avoid both extremes of *biblicism* and *eisegesis* by respecting the tension between the ancient biblical story and our story today. Gerhard Ebeling warns of those who do not:

> The hermeneutic task consists for theology in nothing else but in understanding the Gospel as addressed to contemporary man. Whoever does not expose himself to the tension that entails, betrays both the Gospel and contemporary man alike.[17]

Ebeling says that our task is not so much to understand the text as it is to understand *through* the text.[18] The preacher, therefore, must discover the conversion key that connects the *then* and the *now* so that our stories are seen *through* the story of God. Gerard Sloyan suggests that there is a need "for a grasp of the ancient situation so sure that a transposition to modern categories will be made with ease. This means that the preacher is constantly engaged in biblical studies, thinking of the *now* in terms of the *then*."[19]

Study and Prayerful Imagination

Vatican II's *Constitution on Divine Revelation* urged that preachers "should immerse themselves in the Scriptures by diligent sacred reading and careful study" (Art. 25). There are some who would agree that this is a fine ideal for seminary professors but impractical for the busy minister. While the complaint is somewhat understandable, I believe that the ideal is valid and vital to both effective preaching and caring ministry. Unless you learn how to study and pray over the Scriptures, you soon will become, to paraphrase St. Augustine, an empty preacher of the Word to others because you have not heard the Word first in your heart (Sermon 179, I: PL 38,966). It is not so much a question of the *quantity* but the *quality* of time spent with the Scriptures in our daily pattern of life and preparation of homilies. I will discuss more about this quality of Scripture study in the last chapter when a creative approach to homiletic preparation will be explored. But for now, let us examine two steps that can aid us to think of the *now* in terms of the *then* and view our stories *through* the story of God.

First, there is *study*. As a corrective to fanciful allegorization and eisegesis of the text, *exegesis* is absolutely necessary. Before we start drawing points from the Scripture lesson, we should attempt to get the point the author tried to score for the original hearers and the point the lesson has in a particular liturgical context of the Church year. Exegesis employs the tools of modern biblical scholarship to determine the point that the original author tried to score. When we announce the Gospel, it is always *according to* Matthew, Mark, Luke or John. In this sense, the Bible itself *is* interpretation. To discover what needs, concerns, or context the original author had in mind helps us to discover what the author meant when telling this particular story of God.

Our exegesis should consider the three layers of tradition of a Gospel text which the Pontifical Biblical Commission suggested in its document on the *Historicity of the Gospels:* (1) the actual memories and words of the earthly Jesus; (2) the pre-Gospel oral tradition of the memories and words of Jesus; (3) the redaction of the evangelist which kept "in mind the situation of the churches."[20] Reginald Fuller offers homiletic advice here: "Knowing at which level a particular tradition originated helps greatly in understanding its original meaning, and is therefore important in establishing what the text meant."[21]

It is not enough, however, that our study takes us to discover the original point of view in all three layers of the biblical tradition. Raymond Brown writes: "We cannot bypass historical criticism which is concerned with what a passage meant to the author who wrote it, but the meaning of the Bible goes beyond that. The Bible ceases to be an instrument of comfortable self-affirmation for Christians and the Church when we recognize the tensions between what the word meant and what it means."[22] Our exegesis of the text might challenge us to preach how the particular text was misunderstood or misused by Christians in the history of the Church. Our study of the Scriptures should also include an appreciation of why these particular lessons were chosen at this time in the liturgical year in order to be true to the purpose of the lectionary.

Next, there is *prayerful imagination*. A preacher who has executed the scriptural lessons of a particular Sunday can approach the pulpit with a firm grasp of what the Scripture passages meant to the original listeners but without a clue as to what they mean to the present listeners. If this is the case, then the vital act of the imagination, unfortunately, has been neglected in the homiletic process.

By imagination I am not referring to fantasy but am using the term in Alfred North Whitehead's sense: "Imagination is not to be divorced from the facts; it is a way of illuminating the facts."[23] I am also using the term imagination in the Church's long tradition of prayerful "spiritual reading" (*lectio divina*) where Scripture is read not for information, but for transformation. This is the worthy tradition of direct reading of the Scriptures, where sinners become saints because they picked up the Bible and read it and saw their lives in the new and daring perspective of the story of God. No less a Scripture scholar than Walter Brueggemann reminds us:

> From generation to generation the transmission of the Bible in all its power and vitality has been possible because people with imagination have been sensitive to fresh dimensions of meaning, to new interconnections perceived for the first time, to new glimpses of holiness that lie within the text.[24]

By imagination I refer to the tradition of Augustine, Francis of Assisi, Dag Hammarskjöld, Martin Luther King, Jr., Mother Teresa of Calcutta and so many others down through the ages who read the story of God with open hearts and were transformed.

Whitehead spoke of imagination as youthful. Paul Ricoeur encourages us to develop a "second naiveté"[25] which is a capacity not to disregard our historical-critical facilities, but to allow imagination to speak to us in what he calls a "surplus of meanings." God's story will never become alive to us as preachers if we do not first of all hear it ourselves as addressed to us. God's story is not information gleaned from scriptural commentaries, but a saving word spoken to us now and with our congregation in mind and heart. Elizabeth Achtemeier speaks of the point where the Scripture lesson and the situation of the congregation meet as "the point of crux, of crossing, of crisis. The text interprets the situation; the situation shapes the interpretation. It is at that crucial juncture that the preacher must do the exegesis, and it is at that crisis point that the creative preacher must learn to hold text and situation in delicate balance."[26]

Thus, the preacher must constantly hold *study* and *prayerful imagination* in tension in order to think of the *now* in terms of the *then*. The use of scriptural commentaries for sound exegesis of the text is indispensable, but not the first step in the homiletic process. For creative purposes, which I will discuss in the last chapter, I prefer a direct reading of the Scriptures as a first step. Once the creative process has taken hold, a serious exegetical study can help correct or modify a direct reading, but will not stifle the imaginative reading in faith.

The Uniqueness of God's Story

The God who emerges from the Bible is odd indeed! He is a God who always stretches our boundaries, challenges our wisdom about the way things are, upsets our little theological applecarts. Yet it is this very uniqueness of the God of the Bible that provides us with a way of "seeing in the dark" our own stories. The odd news of God gives us a fresh framework to appreciate our world not as magical but as marvelous, not as evil but as good, not as chaotic but as meaningful. Until we preachers recognize that the God of the Bible is odd and like no other god, we have missed the point of who he is and who we are called to be.

God and History

The God of the Bible is odd because he has a history. The God of the Bible is a living, active God who is involved in the concrete circumstances of life. The Bible is the record of God's wonderful works in history. It is a "memory of historical liberation (exodus) and empowerment (David), of passionate caring-suffering (crucifixion) and the surprise of new life (resurrection)."[27]

We should avoid the mistake, however, of thinking of God's story as identical with human history. Although the Bible describes many events that happened in history, the writers of the Bible should not be understood as modern journalists concerned with the exact chronology and details of history. They were primarily interested in the fact that God was concerned with his people and acted for them and with them. The preacher's task, therefore, primarily is not to highlight the *how* but the *why* of God's activity in history.

For this task, John Shea contributes insight by distinguishing an "interventionist interpretation" from an "intentional interpretation" of God's activity in the Bible.[28] The interventionist interpretation concentrates on *how* God acted in history so that we can observe his coming in the future. The interventionist interpretation views the world as a time of interim, "a time between better times." The best we can do is wait, either actively or passively, for the coming of God in the future, since God's story has already been told in the Bible. Such an interpretation yields a package plan of salvation which respects neither God's freedom to act in ongoing history nor our freedom to read the signs of the times and make responsible decisions.

The intentional interpretation of God's activity in the Bible concentrates not on the *how* of God's activity, but on the *why* of it. It is, in Shea's words, "a tale of God's intentions, his unswerving fidelity to the purposes of his creation." The intentional interpretation does not yield a blueprint to find God's will, but reveals God's intentions so that we can renew our partnership with him. The world is not simplified, but clarified. The world remains ambiguous, mysterious, challenging, and even maddening. But by helping to discern God's intentions (*why* he acted in the Bible story) rather than explaining God's actions (*how* he acted in the Bible story), the preacher invites us to a new way of looking at our world and our lives that is liberating and life-giving.

God and World View

There is a revealing scene in Bertolt Brecht's play *Galileo*. An old cardinal meets to condemn Galileo for his outrageous claim that the earth moves around the sun rather than the traditional way of viewing the world. Galileo's viewpoint devalues man who is the center of God's universe, the cardinal argues. He ends the tirade by shouting, "I won't have it. I won't have it."

While the Bible does not reveal a scientific, post-Copernican view of the world, it does reveal a world view that is different from our own. Preachers who opt for a harmonization of God's world view with our own, rather than a respect for the uniqueness of God's story, are not unlike the old cardinal's refusal to be surprised and contradicted. They have forgotten the challenge of God in the words of the prophet:

> For my thoughts are not your thoughts nor are your ways my ways, says the Lord. As high as the heavens are above the earth, so high are my ways above your ways and my thoughts above your thoughts (Is 55:8–9).

One of the most helpful presentations I have read on how God's world view in the Bible challenges our own is found in Walter Brueggemann's *The Bible Makes Sense*.[29] Brueggemann calls his biblical model the "covenantal-historical way of understanding life and faith." Covenantal refers to the lasting commitment of God to his people, while historical refers to the storehouse of memories of crucial interactions between the covenant partners. Brueggemann describes three modern world views and demonstrates how the covenantal-historical view of the Bible contradicts them.

First, there is the *modern-industrial-scientific model* which relies on performance and reward. Value is placed on people, not for who they are but for what they achieve. It is a *quid pro quo* world view that "puts a premium on what is knowable, manageable, and predictable." The challenge to this model comes from the Bible's covenantal-historical model, where graciousness is valued over what is earned, mystery is embraced rather than everything explained, and transcendence replaces a world where all must be managed. The Bible's viewpoint is that healing and new life take place where all seems broken and impossible. That is why we call it good news.

Second, there is the *existential model* where meaning is found in the loner "who must do his own thing." Here there is no meaning in history, tradition, long-standing communities and institutions. Meaning starts with me, at this present moment, in my current decision. The challenge to this model comes from the Bible's covenantal-historical model where meanings are entrusted to us in our traditions and structures, where life is more than me, but also is found outside my tiny self in communities of meanings, and where the rich memories of the past help me discern continuity so that I can understand the present and hope in the future.

Third, there is the *transcendentalist model* where meaning is found in a serene space outside our messy and complicated world. Brueggemann says that this model has many religious forms "in which pious language and stained-glass windows pretend to screen out the cries of hunger and the groans of injustice." The transcendentalist escapes the historical hurts and sufferings of the real world by escaping to a world beyond. The challenge to this model comes from the Bible's covenantal-historical model where life's ultimate meanings are found in the give-and-take of history, where the incarnation banishes the image of a distant God in a quiet heaven, and where this world is the arena of God's activity and kept promises.

Brueggemann's insights are invaluable for preachers who seek to interpret the way things are. Preachers can easily succumb to the values of the three modern world views rather than preach from the biblical world view. Faulty homiletic viewpoints can be spotted in each of the three models.

First, if we use the *modern-industrial-scientific model* we can preach in a way which somehow gives the impression that God's love can be earned. We can preach in a way that favors only one church, sex, race, nation. If, over the years in a given congregation, we use metaphors and stories that emerge solely from the experience of one denomination, sex, race, nation, then we are undermining, ever so subtly, the good news of the freedom of God's grace. We are preaching not out of the biblical world view, but out of the modern-industrial-scientific model when we tell people that because they are sinners, they are bad. What miracles of healing could occur in our churches if preachers could proclaim with as much passion of God's love and mercy as they often do about our sinfulness!

Second, if we use the *existentialist model* we can preach in a way which somehow gives the impression that the Bible has little to offer us as a fresh framework to view our lives. Some preachers proclaim Jesus as a fire-eating radical Marxist who started his community of faith from his own convictions rather than the traditions of his people. Some have substituted the Bible for *Psychology Today,* while others preach from the *Twin Circle.* Rugged individualism, so at home in American life, must be monitored by the biblical view, where responsible decision-making is a community affair. While we preachers must show how God breaks through in the present moment, we are also called to locate our individual stories in the biblical story of covenant. While current films, humanistic psychology, and political events can help us to read the signs of the times, ultimately they do not save us, but make us realize we are in need of the kind of salvation offered by the God of the Bible.

Third, if we use the *transcendentalist model* we can preach in a way that somehow gives the impression that we have entered a holier world where true peace can be found.

Such preaching encourages manipulative gurus, guilt trips, and escapism. Preachers ignore the incarnational theme of the Bible and preach in stained-glass window tones and pious jargon. Their congregations get the message that this world is evil and the only one worth waiting and praying for is the biblical one of heaven. Such preachers never get into such messy problems as racism, sexism, denominationalism, world hunger, and injustice. After all, what do these have to do with "spirituality"? The people have enough problems as it is; they come to church for peace. But the people of the Bible whom God anoints, invites, confronts, challenges, and loves are not neat, perfect people. They are like us in so many ways. James Sanders says: "It seems that about seventy-five percent of the Bible celebrated the theologem *errore hominum providentia divina:* God's providence works in and through human error and sin."[30] We need to preach from the covenantal-historical model to show how God is willing to take our human limitations for his purposes and meet us not in the sky, but in this world which he called good.

Summary

We are called to preach God's story as found in the covenantal-historical model of the Bible. The story of God in the Scriptures is for Christians *the* story, *the* frame of reference, *the* way of "seeing in the dark." It is God's story that helps us embrace our own pilgrim stories where he still speaks and is there for us.

1. The story of God as presented in the lectionary allows us to proclaim the dying and rising of Christ made present in us through faith and baptism. The story of God, expressed in Jesus and all the prophets, becomes our story as well.

2. We preachers must think of the *now* in terms of the *then.* We offer not merely an explanation of the biblical text, but a transformation for our lives *through* the text.

3. We avoid the extremes of *biblicism* and *eisegesis* by proper *exegesis* and *imaginative, prayerful* readings of the biblical lessons.

4. God's story is a two-edged sword. The uniqueness of God's *covenantal-historical* story calls us to comfort the afflicted and confront the comfortable.

V

The Story of the Listener

At Harvard's 1978 commencement, Alexander Solzhenitzyn delivered a controversial address. The exiled Russian author attacked American democracy whose restrictions, he felt, ensured that "mediocrity triumphs." He chided the United States for a "decline in courage," especially "among the ruling groups and the intellectual elite"—a point that must have ruffled not a few academic gowns. *Time* magazine asked eight distinguished leaders to respond to Solzhenitzyn's rap on Western democracy. Of the eight responses, I found the poet Archibald MacLeish most on target. MacLeish concluded:

> If Solzhenitzyn had talked to us—to a few of his neighbors in that village of Vermont—three or four of those who respect and admire him throughout the country—he would not have spoken those sentences at Harvard. He would have learned that we know who we are and what we have to become. He would have learned that we have not lost our will as a people which makes us true believers in that human spirit for which he means to speak.[1]

There are shades of Aristotle's *Rhetoric* in MacLeish's response. Aristotle recognized the significance of audience analysis when he observed that of the three elements basic to communication—the speaker, the message, and the listener—

it is the listener who determines the speech's end or object. Had Solzhenitzyn truly heard the stories of his listeners, his speech might have resonated with the feelings and convictions that the poet described as authentic.

MacLeish's advice to speak to a few neighbors is a sound rubric for preachers who must first listen to the stories of the congregation before they preach. John Navone reminds us:

> Our storylistening is a precondition for our storytelling, both for the story that our lives will tell and for the many stories that we shall tell about ourselves and our world.[2]

The touchstone of God's pilgrim people as described by Vatican II is dialogue. That is why the Council's documents so often reveal the significance of what is referred to here as the story of the listener. In the *Decree on the Ministry and Life of Priests,* we are urged to "apply the perennial truth of the Gospel to the concrete circumstances of life" (Art. 4). In the *Constitution on the Sacred Liturgy,* the character of the homily, "God's wonderful work," is not simply a past event, but "ever made present and active within us" (Art. 35). The *Instruction* of 1964 insisted that the homily take "into account the mystery which is being celebrated and the particular needs of the hearers" (Art. 54).

I have often cautioned my students not to take too seriously the polite and gracious affirmations their listeners offer after Sunday Mass: "Nice homily." "Thank you for that message." "I really enjoyed your homily today." Such cozy comments hardly constitute an effective feedback system. But I must admit that there is one comment that a preacher hears now and then that not only warms the heart, but gives a fair indication that the story of the listener was heard in the homily: "I felt as though you were speaking directly to me." The listener participated in the story because it was enough like his or her own to spark a link. And, even though the story told belonged to someone else, the listener saw himself or herself as the central character.

The following clues from narrative theology and pastoral homiletics hopefully can lead us to that kind of identification with the story of the listener.

1. The Listener Has a Story Too

In Chapter II we considered Reuel L. Howe's insight that preaching is dialogical. The homily is not a finished monological product communicated from the preacher to the listener, but stories that are shared between them. The caring preacher believes like Sam Keen that "every person has a story to tell. That's what makes a person. There are no autonomous, anonymous, pragmatic individuals."[3]

The tragedy of our technocratic age is that we often get so wrapped up in a noisy, demanding, impersonal world that we forget that each of us has a story to tell. We lose perspective, a center, a way of "seeing in the dark." The "days of our lives," like the television soap opera, seem like an unending series of chaotic events that lead to nowhere.

A modern day parable of how we can lose touch with our story appeared in the *New York Times* on February 29, 1972 (p. 41). The article described Edwin Aldrin as "the second man to set foot on the moon." Aldrin spoke of the rigidly structured training program before his famous flight. It was an ordered training centered entirely outside himself. When he returned to earth to face the significant people of his life, all the orderliness and programmed expectations suddenly vanished. Despite his costly and elaborate training, he had never developed the inner resources and center needed to cope with his life and his times. Indeed, he was chosen to go to the moon in the first place because he appeared to be a well-ordered cog in the space machine. But when he had to face the ordinary challenges of his personal life, he collapsed and had, in his words, "a good old-fashioned American nervous breakdown."

The preacher must not merely respect and retell the story of the listener in the homily, but must give that story a perspective, a center, a way of "seeing in the dark." The preacher must invite the listeners to embrace their unique stories in a way that leads to mystery, possibility, and conversion.

One of the most tragic lines of contemporary literature is spoken by the son at Willy Loman's grave in *Death of a Salesman:* "He never knew who he was." The task of the preacher is to retell the story of the listener in a way that leads to who we really are, and that makes us open to the "mystery of Christ ever made present and active within us."

But remember, before we preachers can retell the story of the listener, we must first of all have ears to hear that story. The preacher must remember the poet and listen "to a few of his neighbors." We preachers can listen to the stories of our listeners both directly and indirectly.

(a) *Directly:* The National Council of Catholic Bishops' thoughtful booklet on pastoral ministry in the United States, *As One Who Serves,* suggests a need for creative dialogue, for directly listening to all people in the pilgrim Church:

> In this process of dialogue the pilgrim Church must be radically open: to listen not only to the people's words but also to their hearts, to welcome the other with respect for dignity and freedom, to discover the elements of truth in the words, lives and experience of others. To dialogue in this spirit of service is to risk disruption of set patterns.[4]

Some of the patterns of preparing a homily have been successfully disrupted in recent years by the use of pastoral feedback and feedforward strategies. These have emerged from many a preacher's conviction that the homily must be dialogical and thereby include the listener as a partner in the preaching event.

A *feedback strategy* is one which allows the preacher to receive reactions and suggestions about the homily that was preached. A *feedforward strategy* is one which includes some listeners in the process of creating a homily.

■ *Written Feedback:* Here the preacher solicits reactions in written form. The feedback sheets can be placed in the pews or on the page of a Sunday bulletin. The congregation is invited to fill out the form and return it with the offering, or take it home to fill it out in more detail and mail it back to the preacher. A feedback form I have found to be most practical and helpful is one by Lowell Erdahl which incorporates suggestions of Reuel Howe's *Partners in Preaching.*[5]

PLEASE HELP YOUR PREACHER

To let your preacher know what his sermons mean to you, please share your responses on this card and return it with the offering. You need not sign your name.
Thank you.

1. What did this sermon say to you?

2. What difference, if any, do you think the message will make in your life?

3. What did the preacher do to help or hinder your communication?

Please use reverse side if needed.

■ *Group Feedback:* Here the preacher invites a small group of people (6-8) to give their reactions to the homily. Many who have worked with group feedback, like Reuel

Howe, suggest that the group make use of a tape recorder for their reactions. This method allows the group to interact more freely and honestly. After the session, the recording is given to the preacher for study. It is wise to have a moderator in the group who is able to guide the participants in a discussion with questions similar to those in the Erdahl feedback form.

■ *Group Feedforward:* Many preachers now invite small groups of people to participate in the preparation of the homily. Parishioners of various ages and levels of faith (even a nonbeliever from time to time) meet with the preacher for about an hour each week. The Scripture lessons for the following week are heard, prayed over, and discussed. The participants offer their own personal experiences of what the readings say to them and also search some commentaries on the Scripture passages in order to understand what the readings meant to the first listeners. Those experienced in working with group feedforward suggest that every few weeks a participant drop out to make room for a new member. Thus, a rich cross-section of listeners is assured.

■ *Special Occasions for Group Feedforward:* There are times when the preacher will want to hear the stories of listeners who will participate in a special occasion liturgy, e.g., wedding, funeral, graduation, etc. I remember sitting in the living room of friends whose mother had just died of cancer. The minister and his wife had come to comfort the family and to plan the funeral service. The minister listened as family members began to tell stories of their mother that revealed her faith and unique personality. Sharing stories of someone we loved is a natural way to cope with death. It is perhaps the first step toward healing and acceptance. These shared stories help us to arrive at a deeper understanding of what his or her life was all about. Because the minister was a caring listener, his funeral homily the next day wonderfully retold the family's stories in the faith-evoking context of God's story.

(b) *Indirectly:* Fred B. Craddock has given us insight into the value of preaching as storytelling by describing preaching as "overhearing the Gospel." In other words, the listener is not confronted directly with a lesson that he or she may turn on or off. Rather, the listener "overhears" and thus participates in an interesting story of someone else that somehow mirrors the listener's own story. Craddock explains:

> It is impossible, as any attender at a play or reader of a book or listener to a story knows, for a speaker to be engaged in narration that is historical, descriptive, third person, and for a hearer to identify, participate, and, if I may say so, be encountered. If the story is the right story, and if the teller narrates with insight and empathetic imagination, conscious of but not occupied with the listener, then the one who overhears will hear.[6]

Craddock developed his theory of "overhearing the Gospel" from Soren Kierkegaard's understanding of indirect communication. It happened that Kierkegaard one day overheard a grandfather explain the meaning of life, death and resurrection to his grandson. The setting was a cemetery where the son stood by his father's grave. Kierkegaard was deeply moved by the conversation because he had the distance needed to participate in the story. Craddock believes that our participation demands the same kind of distancing. Instead of directly confronting the listener with his or her particular story, the preacher indirectly allows the listener distance to "overhear" his or her story in the story of someone else. John Shea writes: "The story is able to meet us where we are at without clubbing us into where we should be. Although the story focuses our minds and hearts, it does not close them down, demanding we move in only one direction."[7] We make the story our own by completing it in a personal way that often leads to a change of heart. Perhaps the reason why many adults claim that they learn so much from listening to homilists preach at children's liturgies is that they are afforded the distance needed to "overhear the Gospel."

In Chapter III it was suggested that the preacher should heed the advice of Faulkner who said that if art is to be relevant to the people of our age, "it must be true" and "loaded with the realities of the human heart." That is why some of the most relevant preaching heard today is not heard from the pulpit, but in the truthful preaching of poets, playwrights, and novelists *overheard*. Their stories are relevant because they emerge from the comedy and tragedy of real people's lives.

How often in a film, a novel, a song, do we "overhear" stories? We are attracted to someone's personal story because it indirectly confronts, teaches, inspires, and sheds light on our own stories. The following is an example of such a story that I "overheard" in a film and placed in a homily:

> The story ends. Or, does it? From childhood we were led to believe that stories do end: "They lived happily ever after." And, we learned to expect that just when all the pieces seemed to fit in a movie, there would roll across the screen the words: "The End." Even our liturgies conclude: "Go, the Mass is ended!"

> A generation ago, William Gibson wrote a play that seemed to end with a "happily ever after" touch: "The Miracle Worker." It was the story of Annie Sullivan, a spitfire governess who survived nine eye operations before she led another blind, deaf, mute girl, Helen Keller, to the miracle of communication. The story seemed to end there, like Luke's story of the blind man: "All the people witnessed it and they too gave praise to God."

> But twenty years later Gibson writes another moving play. It is the story of Annie and Helen twenty years later and it is called *Monday after the Miracle*. The play exposes the white lie that stories end. Ordinary Mondays follow extraordinary Sundays. Like all of us, Annie and Helen live their lives with an old miracle in one hand and the demands of a new day in the other.

2. How To Listen to the Stories of Our Times

Karl Barth once proposed that we ought to prepare our sermons with the Bible in one hand and a newspaper in the other. Barth was referring not simply to the "religious" stories we might find in the newspaper, but to those stories from the economic, political and entertainment world—human interest stories, stories breaking through in people's lives today that, with the eyes of faith, have something to do with the Gospel proclaimed on Sunday. Harvey Cox once said that if God reads *Time* magazine, he does not read first the section on religion, but the section on the world, which is the stage of his activity.[8]

Obviously a preacher cannot be in touch with all the stories of our times, nor should be. There are many stories the preacher can ignore. There are many contemporary tales that provide us pilgrims only with piers and not with bridges to help us on our journey. And, as Sheldon Kopp has reminded us, "a pier is a bridge that goes nowhere."[9] So, then, what kind of stories should the preacher pay close attention to while struggling to hear the story of the listener? Here are some suggestions:

(a) *A story that is similar, yet dissimilar to ours.* Robert McAfee Brown has written:

> If the story is *too dissimilar* to my own, so that I can get no grip upon it, find no point of contact between it and myself, I will become increasingly frustrated with attempts to understand it and . . . I will finally give up in despair.[10]

Preachers whose stories are highly clerical and over-idealized can hardly expect listeners to identify. Catholic tradition has a rich heritage of stories in the lives of the saints. Unfortunately, many of the older stories of the saints were so lofty and removed from people's experiences that they often caused guilt trips rather than led to conversion. For example, hagiographers have determined that many corrections have been made over the years in St. Thérèse's *Journal of a Soul*. Her superiors and friends crossed out much of the humanity, struggle, and humor from the story of the Little Flower.

Brown also writes:

> On the other hand, if the story is *too similar* to my own, so that it introduces nothing I could not have predicted in advance, I will become increasingly frustrated with attempts to maintain interest in it and will give up again, this time not in despair but in boredom.[11]

It is not enough for us to search out contemporary stories similar to our own. The stories we preachers choose should, like the parables of Jesus, open up new doors, provide a different vision, a way of dealing with the concerns and tensions of our lives. John Shea reminds us:

> The stories of Scripture were remembered and today remain memorable because they are similar enough to our lives for us to see ourselves, yet different enough from our lives for us to see new possibilities. They tell us what we want to know and more.[12]

For example, we used to relate to Archie Bunker and his son-in-law Michael. Their battles and ideological differences were similar to our own stories. But in an episode of *All in the Family* where Mike and Gloria appear for the last time, something gloriously new and unexpected takes place. The couple are leaving for California. Gloria rushes out to the car with her baby. Edith runs in tears to the kitchen. The two warriors are left, standing speechless on the front porch. There is a long silence, but it is finally broken when Mike says to Archie in a halting voice. "I know we've had our fights, a lot of them. But before we go, I want you to know, Arch, that I love you and will miss you." Archie raises his hand in a gesture of peace. The old bigot's eyes are flushed with tears.

Here is a story that many of my listeners saw and heard. It had the power to open new doors. It was a way of "seeing in the dark." That is why it was included in my homily about the difficulty of reaching out to others in love and reconciliation.

(b) *A story that reflects our sad yet hopeful times.* There is a bittersweet scene in the film *Sunday, Bloody Sunday.* It is a bright Sunday morning in the British countryside. People depart from a charming church to the music of an organ hymn. A smiling vicar shakes the hands of his congregation. Even the birds chirp a hopeful song. But suddenly the camera shifts its focus to the other side of the street. There, a small gang of mean children scrape the parked cars with pieces of a broken milk bottle. There is an interfacing of both the peaceful and the violent scenes. The director seems to tell us that we live in the middle of things, in the tension between good and evil, hope and sadness.

Our stories should be like that because that is how we experience life. Some homilies reveal only the good news and not the sad. But we do live in a time when people feel the awful absence of God and a terrible sense of anxiety, loneliness, and insecurity. Racism and violence do exist. So does the possibility of a nuclear war. A third of the world go to bed hungry each night. To deny this sad news is to lie. Frederick Buechner comments:

> One wonders if there is anything more crucial for the preacher to do than to obey the sad news of our times by taking into account without equivocation or subterfuge, by speaking out of our times not just what we ought to say about the Gospel, not just what it would appear to be in the interests of the Gospel for us to say, but what we ourselves felt about it, experienced of it.[13]

On the other hand, some homilies speak only of gloom. The hope held out for us by the Gospel of Jesus is muted by the preacher's own cynicism and self-doubt. We invite the people before the Preface: "Lift up your hearts." Does our homily also invite our listeners to lift up their hearts?

A few years ago, while reading the *Baltimore Sun,* I spotted a story that spoke eloquently of the need for hope in our sad times. It was the story of Scharansky, the Russian dissident, and his stirring speech at his trial:

> "I am happy. I am happy that I lived honestly in peace and with my conscience. I never compromised my soul, even under the threat of death.
>
> "For more than 2,000 years the Jewish people, my people, have lived in dispersal. But wherever they are, wherever Jews are found, every year they repeat: 'Next year, in Jerusalem.'
>
> "Now when I am further than ever from my people, from my Avital (his wife's nickname), facing many arduous years of imprisonment, I say, turning to my people, to my Avital: 'Next year, in Jerusalem.'
>
> "Now I turn to the court who is required to confirm a predetermined judgement. To you, I have nothing to say."
>
> The tension was gone.
>
> The dissidents—Jews, Christians and the atheists—wept and applauded and sang the "Hatikvah," the Israeli anthem whose name, translated, means hope.

Scharansky's story became our story in my Sunday homily that week at Baltimore's old Cathedral of the Assumption. The first reading that day was from Isaiah 40:1–5, 9, where, in the sadness of exile, the Israelites heard a song of hope:

> Comfort, give comfort to my people, says your God. Speak tenderly to Jerusalem, and proclaim to her that her service is at an end, her guilt is expiated. . . . Cry out at the top of your voice, Jerusalem, herald of good news.

(c) *A story that attends to the listeners' needs:* The humanistic school of psychology (Maslow, Rogers, *et al.* has described men and women as need-meeting beings who progress through various developmental stages. The preacher's role, according to Vatican II, is to attend to "the particular needs of the hearers." Obviously, no preacher can attend to all the particular needs of a congregation in a single homily. Our listeners are on many different levels of age, education, and faith, and therefore they represent a plethora of needs. The sensitive preacher must continuously wrestle with the question, "Who are my listeners?"

However, over a period of time, a preacher can attend to listeners' needs directly through feedback and feedforward strategies and indirectly through the stories of our times. In novels, films, magazine articles, television shows, newspaper stories, and plays we find a bonanza of stories that reflect people's needs. And while our novelists and poets do not save us, they can often lead us to the knowledge that we are in need of salvation.

Perhaps the most significant need that our literature dramatizes is the need to cope with what the philosophers call "ontological anxiety." Our modern technocratic and impersonal society has produced a people apprehensive about finiteness, perplexed over decisions to be made, upset over an ever-growing ambiguity. That is why today many people are raising the ontological question (Who am I?) before the ethical question (What must I do?). This need to cope with "ontological anxiety" is found, to some degree, in all our listeners, no matter what their age or background. Perhaps this is the reason *Roots* was such a successful television event. People of all ages and races found in the story of Kunta Kinte a way toward self-worth, identification and liberation.

Our anxious age has given us an understanding of the basic needs in terms of acceptance, reconciliation, and affirmation. Herbert Kohl describes this need:

> Our culture creates overwhelming needs in many individuals to be loved, accepted, reassured, confirmed because it creates in them a sense of their own worthlessness and disposability. . . . The over-riding sense that envelops many

people in our culture leads them to a frantic search for confirmation and acceptance. Convinced that there is no core to their own being, no center they can define for themselves, they seek others to care for them, to reassure them of their own worth.[14]

If we preachers listen to the stories of our time, we will be aware that many in the congregation have good reason to despair. But the challenge of the preacher is to invite people to hope and to urge them not to settle for a superficial confirmation in self-worth. The preacher invites the listener to embrace his or her story, as anxious and confusing as it is, because that is the place where the Lord touches us and saves us. Martin Buber tells the tale of the dying Rabbi Zusya who is surrounded by his disciples. They tell him how great he is, a veritable Moses, but the poor rabbi only says: "In the coming world I shall not be asked, 'Why were you not Moses?' They will ask me, 'Why were you not Zusya?' "[15]

The preacher holds the mirror of God's revealing Word in such a manner that the listener sees himself or herself and our world with all the warts of anxiety but also with the firm and loving acceptance of God. The German homileticians have a word for this attendance to the basic human need, *anknüpfungspunkt.* It is the human point of vulnerability where God's Word can take root. In *Five Cries of Youth,* Merton P. Strommen sums up the total goal of the preacher of the Gospel this way:

> ... to convince a person that he is loved by God and is an important member of God's family. When such a message dawns on a person who feels worthless, it is "good news" indeed. His change in perception leads to a new outlook on life; he emerges from the cave of loneliness and comes back into touch with himself, others, and God.[16]

During Eastertime, we hear the transforming story of the disciples on their way to Emmaus. It is a story similar to our own—people on the way who are sad, anxious, confused by the events of their lives. Cleopas and his friend were transformed because the Lord walked with them and dared to ask them: "What are you discussing as you go your way?" Before he said a thing, he listened. He allowed them to tell their own story of conflict and lost hope. Then the Lord placed their story in the context of Scripture, which is the story of God's promise to his people. We preachers must do the same so that our listeners too can exclaim: "Were not our hearts burning inside us as he talked to us on the road and explained the Scriptures to us?"

Summary

Before we preachers can become storytellers, we must become storylisteners. We must not only listen to God's story and our own, but must be sensitive to the story of our listeners. In the words of Karl Rahner: "The preacher should be able to hear his own sermon with the ears of his actual audience."[17]

The preacher must not merely attend to the story of the listener, but must give the story a perspective, a center, a way of "seeing in the dark." The preacher invites the listeners to own their unique stories in a way that leads to transformation.

1. The listener has a story too and it can be heard:
   a. directly, through such strategies as written feedback, group feedback, group feedforward, and special occasion group feedforward;
   b. indirectly, through listening to the stories of our times.

2. The stories of our times that are best suited to preaching are:
   a. stories that are similar, yet dissimilar to ours;
   b. stories that reflect our sad, yet hopeful times;
   c. stories that attend to the listeners' needs.

VI

A Creative Approach

There are many preachers who are open enough to tell their own story, who can intelligently tell God's story, and who care enough to include the listeners' story in their homilies. The struggle comes, however, with trying to integrate all three stories in a creative way.

People have always complained about dull homilies. But our society makes dull preaching even more problematic. Contemporary psychologists often describe our times in terms of boredom or apathy, a subjective condition which makes it difficult to respond, listen, care about. The problem is further complicated by the riveting stimuli that we experience: radio, television, stereo, alcohol, drugs, advertising. Any sensitive preacher today surely feels the demands to preach the Gospel in a creative way.

By creative preaching, I am not referring to gimmickry. A congregation soon grows weary of a preacher with a bag of tricks, especially when they overshadow, rather than highlight the Gospel. We are in the pulpit to minister, not to perform.

The creative preacher is a co-worker with God in his promise to continue to make all things new. We are not like God who produces a *creatio ex nihilo.* We start with the old story of the Gospel, but tell it in a fresh way to these people, in this particular congregation, in these new times. The creative preacher sees relationships between two biblical lessons, the biblical lesson and a current event, theology and life, that others miss. Henri Poincaré speaks of making combinations that "reveal to us unexpected kinship between facts long known but wrongly believed to be strangers to one another."[1] The creative preacher is like the householder that Jesus spoke of who brings out of the storeroom things both new and old (Mt 13:52).

Experience has taught me not to shy away from the "how" of ministry. The minister who cares enough about renewing the Church and the world cannot help but seek aid on how to do it. In preaching workshops, I have observed how preachers who care eagerly seek to learn how to prepare their homilies. There is, of course, no sure method. We must constantly seek out fresh ways to preach. What follows here is one approach to homily preparation that I have found useful. It is based on pastoral experience and some theoretical understandings of creativity.

The Creative Process

How often one hears expressions like "She was born with the gift of music" or "He is a natural artist." Remarks such as these grow out of the myth that there are two kinds of people in the world: creative and non-creative. While much of the creative process remains a mystery, the teachability of the art has been confirmed by scientific investigation which has shown that the average person can almost double his or her ability to think of new ideas in human engineering labs. We are not just creatures who can think analytically and logically, but each of us has the capacity to exercise creative imagination.

Attempts have been made to analyze the process that people travel through on their way to the creative event. Obviously, there is no convenient route that will always guarantee success. But authors like Alex F. Osborn have traced certain paths that creative persons do follow.[2] Osborn suggests four of them: preparation, incubation, illumination, and verification. He does not attempt to reduce the creative process to a simple formula containing these four components that follow a necessary sequence. Osborn seeks merely to distinguish the various activities which make up the creative process.

Preparation

Creative people do not find their masterpieces lying around like shells on the seashore. There is hard work involved, years of practice gathering materials and data, times of frustration and failure.

Osborn offers two basic principles in the idea-finding of the preparation stage.

1. *Deferment of Judgment:* You can think up almost twice as many good ideas (in the same length of time) if you defer judgment until after you have created an adequate checklist of possible leads to solution.

2. *Quantity Breeds Quality:* The more ideas you think up, the more likely you are to arrive at the potentially best leads to solution.[3]

Osborn also stresses the value of *collaboration* in the preparation stage. After an individual has done his or her homework, ideas are reinforced, supplemented, made clearer, by sharing them with others.

When preparation is begun early in the creative process, there is a chance for *selective perception* to take place. Educational psychologists speak of this phenomenon where an individual attends to a certain object and then begins to see that object in places least expected. Selective perception takes place every day. You go to the breakfast table and see in the morning paper an advertisement for Broderick Crawford who is appearing in a summer dinner theater in town. You have not heard his name in a long time, but suddenly Mr. Crawford is there facing you at the gas station where one of your parishioners tells you about seeing him in the play the night before. That night, when you turn on the Late Show, guess who is starring in *Born Yesterday?* Because you selected him from the morning paper for your attention, you are likely to find him in other places during the day.

Jerome Bruner describes creativity as "effective surprise."[4] However he insists that "effective surprise" does not just happen, but is a result of purposeful study. In his *On Knowing: Essays for the Left Hand,* Bruner calls for a discipline of "effective surprise." In other words, early preparation sets the stage for selective perception, for seeing surprisingly new relationships which are at the heart of the creative event.

Incubation

Despite the efforts at preparation and collaboration, creative people come to an inevitable slump in their work. It seems there are too many ideas and surprises with no convenient way of uniting them or choosing the right one for the occasion. It is a time of frustration and fatigue. Osborn points to the value of this period which he calls incubation. He sees it as a time of "purposive relaxation" when the mind's power of association is collating all the data and when "ideas spontaneously well up into our consciousness."[5] Edna Ferber once said that "a story must simmer in its own juice for months or even years before it is ready to serve."

Instead of fighting the stage of incubation, we should make room for it. An early preparation allows quality time for incubation to surface. And when it does, it is advisable to put aside the creative effort for a while. Osborn suggests switching to some physical or mental relaxation. Hobbies, sports, anything that will not absorb too much of your mental energy and attention is encouraged. The change of pace seems to facilitate insights into the creative process.

Illumination

Cartoons usually depict a new idea with a bright light bulb flashing over a character's head. Once again, it must be remembered that the light bulb only *seems* to go on automatically. Preparation and incubation most likely precede the next stage in the creative process: illumination. Illumination is that experience where new ideas begin to emerge or old ideas are seen in a new light. The tension begins to disappear; confidence builds because it seems that something is about to be born. This does not mean that we already have a completed product. Often we have to return to more preparation and incubation, but at least a pattern is emerging and we are sure that we are on the right track.

Often the moments of illumination occur when one is not pushing the creative project. It can take place during quiet moments of prayer, jogging, taking a shower or brushing your teeth in the morning. The long hours of preparation and the necessary stage of incubation have paid off. It is wise to have a pad and pencil or a tape recorder handy to save these ideas when they emerge, lest they slip back into the shadows.

Verification

This is the final stage of the creative process according to Osborn. It is the practical ordering and carrying out of the insights gained in the stage of illumination. Here the creator considers questions of structure, style, language, audience— the creator seeks the most effective way to communicate the insights. Once again, it must be understood that often the creative process is still not complete. In the verification stage, a creator may recognize the need for more preparation before presenting the finished product.

If you have allowed yourself sufficient time in the creative process, you can return for more preparation. Often one hears homilies whose endings lack the same creative approach with which they began. One suspects a lack of time and attention in the verification stage to add the final stylistic touches.

Preparing the Homily

While Osborn's four stages do not pretend to offer a magical formula for creative process, they can provide a preacher with an effective method for preparing Sunday's homily. I do not think that there is a direct ratio between the amount of hours spent in homily preparation with the success of one's preaching. But I do believe that a more creative homily can emerge when a preacher allows quality time for the four stages of the creative process to develop than one who crams one's homiletic preparation on a late Saturday night. A colleague of mine calls the latter type of homily a "Saturday night shot gun special"—it is cheap and not terribly effective. The key to creative homily preparation is to make room for short periods of time during the week, rather than choose one large chunk of time at the end of the week. In that way, the necessary stages of preparation, incubation, illumination, and verification will have adequate time to happen. Also, a preacher will begin to view ministerial experiences with an eye toward preaching. Homily preparation will not be seen as a task performed despite many pastoral duties, but an activity emerging from service to the people.

Vatican II's *Decree on the Ministry and Life of Priests* places the spirituality of the priest in the center of his pastoral work:

> Priests will attain sanctity in a manner proper to them if they exercise their offices sincerely and tirelessly in the Spirit of Christ.

> Since they are ministers of God's Word, they should every day read and listen to that Word which they are required to teach to others. If they are at the same time preoccupied with welcoming this message into their own hearts, they will become ever more perfect disciples of the Lord (Art. 13).

What follows is a working model for homily preparation that is based on the theoretical constructs for creativity we have been considering and one that is nurtured by a preacher's own faith.

Preparation

I have found some old homiletic books that suggest a preacher write out the homily on Monday morning. I have never met the preacher who did follow that rubric. Besides, it is not the best advice, considering what was said about allowing the four stages of the creative process to take their due course. Monday morning is a good time, however, to begin the process. A reading of the Sunday scriptural texts could be the foundation of morning prayer. St. Thomas Aquinas believed that the vocation of the preacher was *contemplare et aliis tradere contemplata:* to contemplate and to share with others the fruit of the contemplation. William Skudlarek refers to this contemplation as "dwelling with the Word":

> This "dwelling with the Word" is the first and indispensable step in preaching it. Unless we hear the Word, there is very little likelihood that we will speak it in a way that others will be able to hear it as a word of life for them. It will be simply "information," interesting perhaps, but most likely boring and irrelevant. Something "back then" and "out there," which has no meaning for their lives.[6]

Keep in mind what was said about *deferment of judgment* in the creative process. Some preachers go immediately to Scripture commentaries and/or homiletic services and make a quick judgment about what they will preach on Sunday. While consulting these resources is a necessary part of the preparation stage, for creative purposes it is wiser to approach the Scripture readings first with prayerful imagination. Later on in the week, after dwelling with the Word and allowing *selective perception* to take place, you could then approach exegetical study. Your study will either confirm or correct your dwelling with the Word.

Simply dwelling over the story of Cleopas and his friend on the road will focus attention on such biblical clues as "walking away from Jerusalem"; "lost hope"; a "stranger" who asks them, "what are you discussing?"; "how slow you are to see what is happening"; "they recognized him in the breaking of the bread"; "they got up immediately and returned to Jerusalem."

During the week, if you have your eyes and ears open, most likely those clues will appear in new ways. For example, you might read an article about the startling rise in the suicide rate among teenagers. You may see a television special about the despair caused by the nuclear arms race. What do these stories have to do with the "lost hope" of Cleopas and his friend? On still another occasion during the week, you might hear the cries of an old woman in a nursing home who comes to reconciliation with herself and the Lord, simply because you asked her, "What is happening to you here?" During the week you might see a film like *Chariots of Fire* that tells the story of men running not away from their goal, but toward it. What do these stories have to do with God's story on Sunday? The creative wrestling is at work.

The selective perception process continues even with stories from the preacher's past. You are studying once again the documents of Vatican II for an adult education discussion group and are impressed with the description of the Bible as a mirror in which we see our lives in a new way. And, once again, the powerful image of the Church as a pilgrim people on a journey reminds you of the disciples on their way to Emmaus.

Keep in mind what was said earlier about the value of collaboration in the preparation stage. Early in the week you should consult some worthwhile Scripture commentaries and homiletic resource books to enhance appreciation of the Sunday Scripture readings. For example, a perusal of Reginald H. Fuller's *Preaching the New Lectionary* will offer up-to-date exegesis that should further fan the flames of creativity. Fuller's remarks about the Emmaus story reflecting the pattern of early Christian worship offers further insight for Sunday's homily.[7]

Many preachers make use of the numerous homiletic services that are on the market to provide a springboard for homiletic ideas. While there is obvious danger in relying on canned homilies for the Gospel message, some of the services do offer homiletic insight, exegetical applications, and contemporary images to help spark a preacher's creative efforts. Here the Canterbury Tales dynamic is at work, where one person's story helps to recall our own stories. Of course one must be selective; not all of the author's examples will prove relevant or worthwhile. The very nature of homiletic services is impersonal. Even if the author uses personal anecdotes, they spring from the author's own story and often do not reflect the story of the preacher who employs the service. If you study a service that includes a complete homily or canned homily outline, you must add your own story and your listener's story and must constantly ask yourself whether or not the convictions and style of the homily can be your own. It seems that the service which does not contain a pre-packaged homily, but rather a helpful exegesis or possible homiletic application, is best suited to the creative process of homily preparation.

Besides collaboration with homiletic resources, you could also concur with various people during the week about the Scripture texts. Some preachers belong to weekly feedforward groups composed of other preachers and/or lay persons who reflect upon the Sunday readings together. Such an experience offers us a good opportunity to make certain that we have included the listeners' story in the homily.

Incubation and Illumination

We should consciously take time out for incubation periods in our busy week in order to get rid of those kinks in our joints and those cobwebs in our heads. Vincent Dwyer, the Trappist priest who has become a guru to many American priests, presents a holistic approach to spirituality which includes the need for regular physical exercise. Jogging, swimming, playing tennis, or even a daily walk with the dog affords a break in our sedentary clerical lives that enriches our capacity for life and service.

Ordinarily, periods of illumination do not last long. Soon

the preacher is back to the hard task of preparing the homily. This is why it is important to grasp the insights when they do occur by jotting down a few notes.

Often what the illumination period allows us to do is to drop many of the homiletic ideas that have occurred during the week. We must develop a sense of relinquishment so that there may emerge one sentence that captures all we wish to say in the homily. There is sound theoretical ground for this stance. Communication experts speak of the phenomenon of *retroactive inhibition,* which is a complicated name for a simple idea. *Retroactive inhibition* means that when we give too much information at one time, we tend to inhibit the necessary information. Listen and watch television commercials carefully and you will realize that there are not three main points, but one single message (Sanka brand *is* real coffee) that sells the product.

Verification

Suppose the sentence that emerges for the homily is: *God leads us to new hope by illuminating the lost hope of our journey.* Once the sentence emerges, it is time to go back to the drawing board in order to plan the homily.

There are those who strongly urge a complete writing out of the text. George R. Fitzgerald has written: "The preacher who doesn't write is in danger of becoming slipshod in style, limited in vocabulary, superficial in thought, and helter-skelter. Writing out the sermon (even if you don't intend to memorize or read it) enhances the possibility of a sharper image. Writing commits you to words and ideas which have been thought through and prayed over."[8]

However, I have heard other homileticians cautioning against writing out one's homily. There is a fear that such a homily will lack spontaneity and become too rigid for an oral communication.

Both sides of the argument merit our attention. It is true that writing does press us into discipline for vocabulary, development, style, and clarity. As much as I cringe when I hear a homily read verbatim, I would still prefer such preaching to a homilist who "gets out there and says a few words to the people," which means saying nothing that was prepared nor prayed over and certainly is never a *few* words. I call these "hamburger helper homilies" because the preacher insults us by not offering quality meat, but mixes a few sentences from the Scripture readings of the day with homiletic morsels that have been pre-packaged and preached many times before. While the read homily lacks spontaneity, at least I am aware that the preacher has prepared it with some deal of care for the people.

But it is also true that writing out a homily means forcing an oral communication event into a written medium. Marshall McLuhan differentiated the two media: the first, intended for the ear, the second, intended for the eye: ". . . writing tends to be a kind of separate or specialist action in which there is little opportunity or call for reaction."[9] In oral communication, such personal elements as spontaneity, sincerity and emphasis are quickly grasped by the listeners. There is a chance for immediate interaction that written communication does not afford.

We just do not talk the way we write. For example, when we talk, we tend to use contractions, shorter sentences, and we do not always have the exact word ready, which adds a natural hesitation to our speech. How often we are put off by the preacher whose words flow so glibly and perfectly from a read or memorized manuscript that it seems as though we are listening to a cold, clerical computer. There is a lack of naturalness. There seems little involvement with where we are at or who we are. Archbishop Fulton Sheen once spoke of the woman who remarked to a young priest who had just read a sermon verbatim: "If *you* can't remember it, how am *I* supposed to remember it?"

There must be a middle-way that captures the positive elements from both written and oral preparation, a way that may be called "planned spontaneity." In other words, in the verification stage of the creative process, the homilist should plan to execute the homily well, but in a way that maintains the spontaneous elements of an oral and narrative style.

If, as I have suggested in this text, an ideal homily contains the stories of the preacher, God, and the listener, the verification stage of preparation should consider these three stories.

Planned Spontaneity

For their speeches, the ancient Greeks employed *topoi* or special categories to expand the creative process and add interest to their subject. The three story model provides the preacher with *topoi* that help facilitate homiletic preparation.

Take the one sentence that sums up the homily and consider it in the light of the three stories of preacher, God, and listener. Take each of these stories and write out a few sentences, phrases, key words on each, keeping in mind always the one sentence that sums up the homily. Do it on three separate sheets of paper. Then take each of the papers and "talk out" your reflection on each story. Some find a tape recorder useful here. In his *Preaching for Today,* Clyde E. Fant refers to this "talking out" of the homily as a "rough oral draft":

> The composition is oral, not written, and the difference can be plainly heard in the final product. Verbal fluency will jump dramatically using this method. And rather than practicing on your audience, you are practicing on yourself.[10]

In the "talking out" stage, key phrases, transitions, concrete examples, stories, and direction sentences will begin to take shape. You will decide, for example, with which story to begin. I usually prefer to begin with the story of the listener or the story of the preacher. Starting here usually is more of an attention getter and a smoother introduction to God's story. Fred B. Craddock speaks of this method as "inductive movement" and points to its advantages over a "deductive movement" in preaching:

> Thus far the attempt has been made to say that inductive movement in preaching corresponds to the way people ordinarily experience reality and to the way life's problem-solving activity goes on naturally and casually. It has been urged that this method respects rather than insults the hearer and it leaves him the freedom and hence the obligation to respond. In addition, unfolding or unrolling the sermon in this fashion sustains interest by means of that anticipation built into all good narration.[11]

You should allow for a repetition of key words and especially the key sentences of the homily as it is talked out. While repetition is monotonous in the written medium, it is essential for the oral event.

Next, jot down the natural story line of the scriptural pericope to allow a narrative shape to emerge from the homily, rather than drawing points out of the biblical story for explanation.

For example, in the Lucan account of the Emmaus story, notice the natural story line: (1) *Lost hope:* the disciples are walking away from their dreams because the one they had hoped in is gone; (2) *Interpretation:* a stranger interprets the sad events through the Scriptures; (3) *New hope:* this comes in the recognition of the Lord in the breaking of the bread and in their remembrance of his interpretation of their lost hope.

The homily begins, therefore, with what Anglicans call "from the bottom" (the story of the preacher or listener), rather than "from the top" (the story of God). It begins with our own story of *lost hope* and considers a film, a news account, a personal experience of people today walking away from a dream because they believe the dream is dead. The preacher dares to speak of lost hope today—how our leaders have lost courage; how despair surrounds us; how even the Lord at times seems illusive and fleeting in our lives.

The homily then moves toward *interpretation* and shows

how God reveals himself in the midst of lost hope and sometimes through a stranger who dares to tell us the sad news before telling us the good news. You show how Jesus led the disciples from logic and lost hope to communion and new hope by challenging them to realize that "Christ had to suffer." You remind the listeners of how the Bible, with its embrace of both the tragic and joyful in life, is a mirror in which we see ourselves.

The homily concludes with an invitation to *new hope*, which might emerge in the story of a person who until now was a stranger to us. His or her story of not walking away from lost dreams but facing them in the light of God's story gives us both courage and challenge for our own journey.

You now have a structure for the homily which follows the natural story line of the Scripture story. Now talk out the homily in this story-like manner until it is ready to preach. When a homily follows such a natural story line and has been talked out in an oral style of communication, you need not turn to memorization or a flat reading from a written text. The homily will be as natural to preach as a story is to tell.

Such a homily, which is the creative fruit of study and prayer, tradition and conviction, will offer more than "points to be understood." It will help us to get the point of the Scripture reading, to recognize the Lord in the breaking of the bread, and to discern the Lord walking with us. Such a homily will make our hearts burn and help us to return to Jerusalem.

Summary

The creative preacher is a co-worker with God in his promise to make all things new. The creative preacher knows that God works through our efforts which demand a discipline for effective surprise. The creative discipline that has been suggested here is one that recognizes the four stages of preparation, incubation, illumination, and verification. It calls for planned spontaneity, which is the fruit of an oral draft and a natural story line.

When we reflect upon the creative homily, we can turn to the following checklist:

1. *Preparation:* There is nothing magical about creative homilies. They are the products of work and prayer. They begin with disciplined efforts of preparation. Praying over the Scriptures early in the week allows us to dwell with the Word so that selective perception begins to take place. We begin to relate the clues of the Scripture readings with the events of the week. Collaboration with others, Scripture commentaries, and homiletic resources continue the creative process.

2. *Incubation:* The preacher allows quality time for physical relaxation and quiet reflection to help facilitate the creative process.

3. *Illumination:* Moments of illumination do not last long, so insights are jotted down on note pads for further use. The preacher reviews and reflects until one clear sentence emerges that best captures the Gospel message.

4. *Verification:* The preacher develops the homily with planned spontaneity. We talk out the homily through the stories of preacher, God, and listener until we are able to deliver the homily as a story and in a spontaneous, oral style.

Notes

Introduction

1. Roger R. Rousseau, "From the Pulpit," *Columbia*, XXXVIII (May 1958), p. 25.
2. Pittsburgh Worship Commission, *The Spirit and Truth* (Pittsburgh: Worship Commission, December 1971), p. 3.
3. Andrew M. Greeley, *Crisis in the Church* (Chicago: Thomas More Press, 1979), p. 60.
4. *Ibid.,* p. 58.
5. Charles Smyth, *The Art of Preaching* (London: SPCK, 1964), p. 60.
6. N. M. Neal, *Medieval Preachers and Medieval Preaching* (London: J. C. Mozley, 1856), pp. xiv–xv.
7. Clyde E. Fant, *Preaching for Today* (New York: Harper and Row, 1975), p. 7.
8. Payne Best, *The Venlo Incident* (London: Hutchinson, 1950), p. 180.
9. As quoted in John Burke, *Gospel Power* (New York: Alba House, 1978), p. ix.
10. Benjamin S. Bloom, *Taxonomy of Education Objectives* (New York: Longmans, Green, 1956).

Chapter I

1. Oscar Cullmann, *Vatican Council II, The New Direction* (New York: Harper and Row, 1968), p. 99.
2. Aidan Kavanaugh, O.S.B. "The Council, The Constitution and Liturgical Reform," *The Impact of Vatican II*, ed. by John Ford (St. Louis: Herder Book Company, 1966), p. 15.
3. Frank B. Norris, S.S., "Preaching the Word of God," *The Challenge of the Council: Person, Parish, World* (Washington, D.C.: The Liturgical Conference, 1964), p. 218.

4. William O'Shea, S.S., "The Sermon Is Part of the Mass," *The Homiletic and Pastoral Review,* LX (March 1960), p. 517.

5. Richard A. Jensen, *Telling the Story* (Minneapolis: Augsburg, 1980), p. 86.

6. O'Shea, p. 523.

7. C. H. Dodd, *The Apostolic Preaching and Its Developments* (New York: Harper and Brothers, 1962), pp. 7–35.

8. J.A. Jungmann, S.J., *Labone Nouvelle et Notre Predication* (Ratisbone, 1936).

9. Gerard S. Sloyan, "Preaching at Mass," in *North American Liturgical Week Proceedings, 1963* (Washington, D.C.: Liturgical Conference, 1964), p. 193.

10. Saint Justin Martyr, "The First Apology," in *Fathers of the Church,* trans. by Thomas B. Falls, ed. by Ludwig Schopp, VI (Washington, D.C.: The Catholic University of America Press, 1948), pp. 106–107.

11. John Burke, O.P., "The Development of the Theology of the Liturgical Sermon in the Formation of the Constitution of the Sacred Liturgy of the Second Vatican Council" (Unpublished S.T.D. dissertation, Catholic University of America, 1968), p. 221.

12. Norris, p. 219.

13. A. Bugnini, C.M. and C. Braga, C.M., eds., *The Commentary on the Sacred Liturgy* (New York: Benziger Brothers, 1965), p. 564.

14. Raymond E. Brown, S.S., "Hermeneutics," *The Jerome Biblical Commentary,* ed. by Raymond E. Brown, S.S., Joseph A. Fitzmyer, and Roland E. Murphy, O.Carm. (Englewood Cliffs: Prentice-Hall, 1969), p. 619.

15. James White, *Christian Worship in Tradition* (Nashville: Abingdon, 1976), p. 139.

16. Sloyan, p. 193.

17. Pope Paul VI, *On Evangelization In The Modern World* (Washington, D.C.: Publications Office of the United States Catholic Conference, 1976), p. 22.

Chapter II

1. Sallie TeSelle, *Speaking in Parables* (Philadelphia: Fortress Press, 1975).

2. Johann Baptist Metz and Jean-Pierre Jossua, eds., *The Crisis of Religious Language* (New York: Herder and Herder, 1973), p. 85.

3. *Ibid.*

4. John Dominic Crossan, *In Parables* (New York: Harper and Row, 1973).

5. Metz, p. 88.

6. Urban T. Holmes III, *Ministry and Imagination* (New York: Seabury, 1976), p. 165.

7. John Navone, S.J., *The Jesus Story: Our Life as Story in Christ* (Collegeville: The Liturgical Press, 1979), p. 41.

8. Sheldon B. Kopp, *If You Meet the Buddha on the Road, Kill Him!* (New York: Bantam Books, 1972), p. 21.

9. Marshall McLuhan, *Understanding Media: The Extensions of Man* (New York: Signet Books, 1964).

10. Robert Béla Wilhelm, "How Tales Are Told," *Liturgy* (May 1974, Vol. 19, No. 5), p. 3.

11. Richard A. Jensen, *Telling the Story* (Minneapolis: Augsburg Publishing House, 1980), p. 129.

12. Amos N. Wilder, *Jesus' Parables and the War of Myths* (Philadelphia: Fortress Press, 1982), p. 83.

13. David James Randolph, *The Renewal of Preaching* (Philadelphia: Fortress Press, 1969), p. 97.

14. Milton Crum, Jr., *Manual on Preaching* (Valley Forge: Judson Press, 1977), p. 26.

15. Reginald H. Fuller, *The Use of the Bible in Preaching* (Philadelphia: Fortress Press, 1981), p. 38.

16. James William McClendon, Jr., *Biography as Theology* (Nashville: Abingdon, 1974).

17. Henri J.M. Nouwen, *Creative Ministry* (Garden City: Doubleday, 1971), p. 37.

18. Reuel L. Howe, *Partners in Preaching* (New York: Seabury, 1967), p. 5.

19. Frederick Buechner, *Telling the Truth: The Gospel as Tragedy, Comedy and Fairy Tale* (New York: Harper and Row, 1977), p. 8.

Chapter III

1. Pope Paul VI, "Address to the Members of the Consilium de Laicis" (October 2, 1974): *AAS* 66 (1974), p. 568.

2. Saint Teresa of Jesus, *The Complete Works of Saint Teresa of Jesus,* trans. and ed. by E. Allison Peers from the critical edition of P. Silverio de Santa Teresa, O.C.D., published in three volumes (New York: Sheed and Ward, 1966), p. 209.

3. Edward Schillebeeckx, *Christ the Sacrament of the Encounter with God* (New York: Sheed and Ward, 1966), p. 209.

4. Eugene A. Walsh, S.S., *Talking with Adults* (Glendale: Pastoral Arts Associates, 1980), p. 164.

5. Hans Küng, *Truthfulness: The Future of the Church* (New York: Sheed and Ward, 1968) pp. 16–17.

6. *Ibid.,* pp. 20–21.

7. Pope Paul VI, *On Evangelization in the Modern World* (Washington, D.C.: United States Catholic Conference, 1975), p. 57.

8. *Ibid.*

9. John B. Sheerin, C.S.P., "In My Opinion," in *Preaching Today* (September–October 1972), Volume 6, Number 5, pp. 2–3.

10. Gerard S. Sloyan, "How Do I Know What I Think Till I Hear What I Say?" (Washington, D.C.: The Liturgical Conference, Inc., 1970), p. 2.

11. William Faulkner, "Nobel Prize Acceptance Speech" Caedmon record 1035; *Eugene O'Neill,* Nine Plays (Modern Library, Random House). Introduction by Joseph Wood Krutch, p. xvii.

12. Myron R. Chartier, *Preaching as Communication* (Nashville: Abingdon, 1981), p. 33.

13. Henri Nouwen, *The Wounded Healer* (Garden City: Doubleday, 1972), p. xiv.

14. Henri Nouwen, *Creative Ministry* (Garden City: Doubleday, 1971), p. 35.

15. H. Grady Davis, *Design for Preaching* (Fortress Press: Philadelphia, 1968), p. 13.

Chapter IV

1. James A. Sanders, *God Has a Story Too* (Philadelphia: Fortress Press, 1979), p. 2.

2. John Reumann, "A History of Lectionaries: From the Synagogue at Nazareth to Post-Vatican II," *Interpretation* (Vol. XXXI, April 1977, No. 2), p. 117.

3. Eugene A. Walsh, S.S., *Talking With Adults* (Glendale: Pastoral Arts Associates of North America, 1980), p. 165.

4. William Skudlarek, O.S.B., *The Word in Worship* (Nashville: Abingdon, 1981), pp. 33–34.

5. As quoted and used for the theme of Fred B. Craddock's *Overhearing the Gospel* (Nashville: Abingdon, 1978).

6. Walter Brueggemann, *The Bible Makes Sense* (Winona: St. Mary's College Press, 1978), p. 10.

7. From "Introduction" to *Lectionary for Mass* (New York: Catholic Book Publishing Company, 1970), p. 9.

8. Gerard S. Sloyan, "The Lectionary as a Context for Interpretation," *Interpretation* (Vol. XXXI, April 1977, No. 2), p. 135.

9. *Ibid.,* p. 133.

10. Justo L. Gonzalez and Catherine G. Gonzalez, *Liberation Preaching* (Nashville: Abingdon, 1980).

11. Sloyan, p. 136.

12. Lloyd R. Bailey, "The Lectionary in Critical Perspective," *Interpretation* (Vol. XXXI, April 1977, No. 2), p. 146.

13. Skudlarek, pp. 41–42.

14. Martin Buber, *Tales of the Hasidim,* trans. by Olga Marx (Schocken Books, Inc., 1957), pp. v–vi.

15. Gerhard Ebeling, *God and Word* (Philadelphia: Fortress Press, 1966), p. 40.

16. Bernard Cooke, *Ministry to Word and Sacraments* (Philadelphia: Fortress Press, 1976), p. 320.

17. Gerhard Ebeling, *Word and Faith* (Philadelphia: Fortress Press, 1963), p. 11.

18. *Ibid.,* p. 431.

19. Gerard S. Sloyan, "How Do I Know What I Think Till I Hear What I Say?" (Washington, D.C.: The Liturgical Conference, Inc., 1970), p. 3.

20. Pontifical Biblical Commission on the *Historicity of the Gospels,* April 21, 1964; Latin and English in CBQ 26 (1964) pp. 299–312; *AAS* 56 (1964) pp. 712–18; Commentary of J.A. Fitzmyer, *TS* 25 (1964) pp. 386–408.

21. Reginald H. Fuller, *The Use of the Bible in Preaching* (Philadelphia: Fortress Press, 1981), pp. 24–25.

22. Raymond E. Brown, S.S., *The Critical Meaning of the Bible* (New York: Paulist Press, 1981), p. 23.

23. Alfred North Whitehead, *The Aims of Education and Other Essays* (New York: Macmillan, 1929), p. 139.

24. Brueggemann, pp. 32–33.

25. Paul Ricoeur, *Interpretation Theory: Discourse and the Surplus of Meaning* (Fort Worth: Texas Christian University Press, 1976), p. 75.

26. Elizabeth Achtemeier, *Creative Preaching* (Nashville: Abingdon, 1980), p. 56.

27. Brueggemann, p. 19.

28. John Shea, *Stories of God* (Chicago: The Thomas More Association, 1978), pp. 89–103.

29. Brueggemann, pp. 10–27.

30. Sanders, p. 135.

Chapter V

1. *Time,* June 26, 1978, p. 21.

2. John Navone, S.J., *The Jesus Story: Our Life as Story in Christ* (Collegeville: The Liturgical Press, 1980), p. 130.

3. Sean Keen and Anne Valley Fox, *Telling Your Story* (New York: Doubleday, 1973), p. 8.

4. The Bishops' Committee on Priestly Life and Ministry of the National Conference of Catholic Bishops, *As One Who Serves* (Washington, D.C.: United States Catholic Conference, 1977), pp. 16–17.

5. Lowell Erdahl, *Better Preaching: Evaluating the Sermon* (St. Louis: Concordia, 1977), p. 32.

6. Fred B. Craddock, *Overhearing the Gospel* (Nashville: Abingdon, 1978), pp. 118–119.

7. John Shea, *Stories of Faith* (Chicago: Thomas More Press, 1980), p. 114.

8. Harvey Cox, *God's Revolution and Man's Responsibility* (Valley Forge: Judson Press, 1965), p. 31.

9. Sheldon B. Kopp, *If You Meet the Buddha on the Road, Kill Him!* (New York: Bantam, 1972), p. 10.

10. Robert McAfee Brown, "My Story and 'The Story,'" *Theology Today,* Vol. XXXII, No. 2, July 1975, p. 166.

11. Brown, p. 166.

12. Shea, p. 89.

13. Frederick Buechner, *Telling the Truth: The Gospel as Comedy, Tragedy and Fairy Tale* (New York: Harper and Row, 1977), p. 7.

14. Herbert Kohl, *Half the House* (New York: Bantam Books, Inc., 1974), pp. 48–49.

15. Martin Buber, *Tales of the Hasidim,* trans. by Olga Marx (Schocken Books, Inc., 1957), p. 251.

16. Merton P. Strommen, *Five Cries of Youth* (New York: Harper and Row, 1974), p. 26.

17. Karl Rahner, ed., *Concilium,* Vol. 33, *The Renewal of Preaching,* trans. by Theodore L. Weston (New York: Paulist Press, 1968), p. 1.

Chapter VI

1. Quoted from Jerome Bruner, *On Knowing: Essays for the Left Hand* (Cambridge: The Belknap Press of Harvard University, 1965), p. 19.
2. Alex S. Osborn, *Applied Imagination* (New York: Charles Scribner's Sons, 1953), p. 315.
3. *Ibid.,* p. 124.
4. Bruner, p. 18.
5. Osborn, p. 314.
6. William Skudlarek, O.S.B., *The Word in Worship* (Nashville: Abingdon, 1981), pp. 52-53.
7. Reginald H. Fuller, *Preaching the New Lectionary* (Collegeville, Minnesota, 1971), p. 181.
8. George R. Fitzgerald, C.S.P., "Preaching From Alpha to Omega," in *New Catholic World* (Vol. 222, No. 1323, May/June 1978), p. 113.
9. Marshall McLuhan, *Understanding Media: The Extensions of Man* (New York: The McGraw-Hill Book Company, 1964), p. 82.
10. Clyde E. Fant, *Preaching for Today* (New York: Harper and Row, 1975), p. 120.
11. Fred B. Craddock, *As One Without Authority* (Nashville: Abingdon, 1971), p. 66.

Bibliography

Achtemeier, Elizabeth, *The Old Testament and the Proclamation of the Gospel.* Westminster, Philadelphia, 1973.
———, *Creative Preaching.* Abingdon, Nashville, 1980.
Babin, David E., *Week In and Week Out.* Seabury, New York, 1966.
Bartow, Charles L., *The Preaching Moment.* Abingdon, Nashville, 1980.
Bishops' Committee on Priestly Life and Ministry, *Fulfilled in Your Hearing: The Homily in the Sunday Assembly.* United States Catholic Conference, Washington, D.C., 1982.
Brilioth, Yngve, *A Brief History of Preaching.* Fortress Press, Philadelphia, 1965.
Brown, Raymond E., *The Critical Meaning of the Bible.* Paulist Press, New York, 1981.
Browne, Robert C., *The Ministry of the Word.* Fortress Press, Philadelphia, 1976.
Brueggemann, Walter, *The Bible Makes Sense.* St. Mary's Press, Winona, Minn., 1977.
Buechner, Frederick, *Telling the Truth: The Gospel as Tragedy, Comedy and Fairy Tale.* Harper & Row, San Francisco, 1977.
———, *Peculiar Treasures: A Biblical Who's Who.* Harper & Row, San Francisco, 1979.
Burke, John, *Gospel Power: Toward the Revitalization of Preaching.* Alba House, New York, 1978.
Chartier, Myron R., *Preaching as Communication,* Abingdon, Nashville, 1981.

Cooke, Bernard, *Ministry to Word and Sacraments.* Fortress Press, Philadelphia, 1976.

Craddock, Fred B., *As One Without Authority.* Abingdon, Nashville, 1971.

———, *Overhearing the Gospel.* Abingdon, Nashville, 1978.

Crum, Minton, *Manual on Preaching.* Judson, Valley Forge, Pa., 1977.

Curran, Charles, *The Crisis in Priestly Ministry.* Fides, Notre Dame, Ind., 1972, chapter 3.

Davis, H. Grady, *Design for Preaching.* Fortress Press, Philadelphia, 1971.

Duke, Robert W., *The Sermon as God's Word.* Abingdon, Nashville, 1980.

Ebeling, Gerhard, *Word and Faith.* Fortress Press, Philadelphia, 1963.

———, *God and Word.* Fortress Press, Philadelphia, 1966.

Fant, Clyde E., *Preaching for Today.* Harper & Row, New York, 1975.

Fischer, Edward, *Everybody Steals from God.* University of Notre Dame Press, Notre Dame, Ind., 1977.

Fitzgerald, George R., *A Practical Guide to Preaching.* Paulist Press, New York, 1980.

Fuller, Reginald H., *The Use of the Bible in Preaching.* Fortress Press, Philadelphia, 1981.

Funk, Robert W., *Language, Hermeneutic, and Word of God.* Harper & Row, New York, 1966.

Gonzalez, Justo L., and Catherine G., *Liberation Preaching.* Abingdon, Nashville, 1980.

Grasso, Domenico, *Proclaiming God's Message.* University of Notre Dame Press, Notre Dame, Ind., 1965.

Hall, Thor, *The Future Shape of Preaching.* Fortress Press, Philadelphia, 1971.

Holland, DeWitte T., *The Preaching Tradition.* Abingdon, Nashville, 1981.

Howe, Reuel L., *The Miracle of Dialogue,* Seabury Press, New York, 1963.

———, *Partners in Preaching.* Seabury Press, New York, 1967.

Jabusch, Willard F., *The Person in the Pulpit*. Abingdon, Nashville, 1980.

Jackson, J.J., editor, *Communication: Learning for Churchmen*. Abingdon, Nashville, 1968.

———, *Television, Radio, Film for Churchmen*, Abingdon, Nashville, 1969.

———, *Audiovisual Facilities and Equipment for Churchmen*. Abingdon, Nashville, 1970.

Jensen, Richard A., *Telling the Story*. Augsburg, Minneapolis, 1980.

Jungmann, Joseph A., *Announcing the Word of God*. Herder & Herder, New York, 1967.

Keck, Leander E., *The Bible in the Pulpit*. Abingdon, Nashville, 1978.

———, and G. M. Tucker, "Exegesis" in *The Interpreter's Dictionary of the Bible*. Abingdon, Nashville, 1976, Supplementary Volume, pp. 296–303.

Killinger, John, *The Centrality of Preaching in the Total Task of the Ministry*. Word Books, Waco, Texas, 1969.

Lowry, Eugene L., *The Homiletic Plot*. John Knox Press, Atlanta, 1980.

Massey, James Earl, *Designing the Sermon*. Abingdon, Nashville, 1980.

Metz, Johann Baptist & Jossua, Jean-Pierre, editors, *The Crisis of Religious Language*. Herder & Herder, New York, 1973, Concilium #85.

Milner, Paulinus, *The Ministry of the Word*. The Liturgical Press, Collegeville, Minn., 1967.

Mitchell, Henry H., *The Recovery of Preaching*. Harper & Row, New York, 1977.

Murphy, Roland, *Theology, Exegesis and Proclamation*. Herder & Herder, New York, 1971, Concilium #70.

Nouwen, Henri J.M., *Creative Ministry*. Doubleday, Garden City, N.Y., 1971.

Paul VI, *On Evangelization in the Modern World*. Publications Office of the United States Catholic Conference, Washington, D.C., 1976.

Pennington, Chester, *God Has a Communication Problem: Creative Preaching Today.* Hawthorn Books Inc., New York, 1967.

Rahner, Karl, *The Word, Readings in Theology.* P.J. Kennedy & Sons, New York, 1964.

————, *Renewal of Preaching.* Paulist Press, New York, 1968, Concilium #33.

Randolph, David James, *The Renewal of Preaching.* Fortress Press, Philadelphia, 1969.

Rice, Charles L., *Interpretation and Imagination.* Fortress Press, Philadelphia, 1970.

Sanders, James A., *God Has a Story Too,* Fortress Press, Philadelphia, 1979.

Shea, John, *Stories of God.* The Thomas More Press, Chicago, 1978.

————, *Stories of Faith.* The Thomas More Press, Chicago, 1980.

Sittler, Joseph, *The Anguish of Preaching.* Fortress Press, Philadelphia, 1966.

Skudlarek, William, *The Word of Worship.* Abingdon, Nashville, 1981.

Steimele, Edmund; Neidenthal, Morris; Rice, Charles, *Preaching the Story.* Fortress Press, Philadelphia, 1980.

Sweazey, George E., *Preaching the Good News.* Prentice Hall, Englewood Cliffs, N.J., 1976.

Von Allmen, Jean-Jacques, *Preaching and Congregation.* John Knox Press, Richmond, Va., 1962.

Walsh, Eugene, *Talking with Adults.* Pastoral Arts Associates, Glendale, Ariz., 1980.